THE GREEK TRAGEDY
IN NEW TRANSLATIONS

GENERAL EDITOR   William Arrowsmith
CO-EDITOR   Herbert Golder

AESCHYLUS: **Prometheus Bound**

AESCHYLUS

Prometheus Bound

Translated by
JAMES SCULLY
and
C. J. HERINGTON

OXFORD UNIVERSITY PRESS
New York   Oxford

OXFORD UNIVERSITY PRESS

Oxford   New York   Toronto
Delhi   Bombay   Calcutta   Madras   Karachi
Petaling Jaya   Singapore   Hong Kong   Tokyo
Nairobi   Dar es Salaam   Cape Town
Melbourne   Auckland

and associated companies in
Berlin   Ibadan

First published in 1975 by Oxford University Press, Inc.,
198 Madison Avenue, New York, New York 10016-4314
First issued as an Oxford University Press paperback, 1989

Oxford is a registered trademark of Oxford University Press

Library of Congress Cataloging-in-Publication Data
Aeschylus.
[Prometheus bound. English]
Prometheus bound / Aeschylus ; translated by James Scully and C.J. Herington.
p.   cm.—(The Greek tragedy in new translations)
ISBN 13 978-0-19-506165-9 (pbk.)
ISBN 0-19-506165-9 (pbk.)
1. Prometheus (Greek mythology)—Drama.
I. Scully, James.   II. Herington, C.J.   III. Title.   IV. Series.
PA3827.P8S3   1989   882'.01—dc20   89–22868   CIP

20 19 18 17 16
Printed in the United States of America

EDITOR'S FOREWORD

The Greek Tragedy in New Translations is based on the conviction that poets like Aeschylus, Sophocles, and Euripides can only be properly rendered by translators who are themselves poets. Scholars may, it is true, produce useful and perceptive versions. But our most urgent present need is for a *re-creation* of these plays—as though they had been written, freshly and greatly, by masters fully at home in the English of our own times. Unless the translator is a poet, his original is likely to reach us in crippled form: deprived of the power and pertinence it must have if it is to speak to us of what is permanent in the Greek. But poetry is not enough; the translator must obviously *know* what he is doing, or he is bound to do it badly. Clearly, few contemporary poets possess enough Greek to undertake the complex and formidable task of transplanting a Greek play without also "colonializing" it or stripping it of its deep cultural difference, its remoteness from us. And that means depriving the play of that crucial *otherness* of Greek experience—a quality no less valuable to us than its closeness. Collaboration between scholar and poet is therefore the essential operating principle of the series. In fortunate cases scholar and poet co-exist; elsewhere we have teamed able poets and scholars in an effort to supply, through affinity and intimate collaboration, the necessary combination of skills.

An effort has been made to provide the general reader or student with first-rate critical introductions, clear expositions of translators' principles, commentary on difficult passages, ample stage directions, and glossaries of mythical and geographical terms encountered in the plays. Our purpose throughout has been to make the reading of the plays as vivid as possible. But our poets have constantly tried to remember that they were translating plays—plays meant to be produced, in language that actors could speak, naturally and with dignity. The poetry aims at being dramatic poetry and realizing itself in words and actions that are both speakable and playable.

Finally, the reader should perhaps be aware that no pains have been spared in order that the "minor" plays should be translated as carefully and brilliantly as the acknowledged masterpieces. For the Greek Tragedy in New Translations aims to be, in the fullest sense, new. If we need vigorous new poetic versions, we also need to see the plays with fresh eyes, to reassess the plays for ourselves, in terms of our own needs. This means translations that liberate us from the canons of an earlier age because the translators have recognized, and discovered, in often neglected works, the perceptions and wisdom that make these works ours and necessary to us.

A NOTE ON THE SERIES FORMAT

If only for the illusion of coherence, a series of thirty-three Greek plays requires a consistent format. Different translators, each with his individual voice, cannot possibly develop the sense of a single coherent style for each of the three tragedians; nor even the illusion that, despite their differences, the tragedians share a common set of conventions and a generic, or period, style. But they can at least share a common approach to orthography and a common vocabulary of conventions.

1. *Spelling of Greek Names*

Adherence to the old convention whereby Greek names were first Latinized before being housed in English is gradually disappearing. We are now clearly moving away from Latinization and toward precise transliteration. The break with tradition may be regrettable, but there is much to be said for hearing and seeing Greek names as though they were both Greek and new, instead of Roman or neo-classical importations. We cannot of course see them as wholly new. For better or worse certain names and myths are too deeply rooted in our literature and thought to be dislodged. To speak of "Helene" and "Hekabe" would be no less pedantic and absurd than to write "Aischylos" or "Platon" or "Thoukydides." There are of course borderline cases. "Jocasta" (as opposed to "Iokaste") is not a major mythical figure in her own right; her familiarity in her Latin form is a function of the fame of Sophocles' play as the tragedy *par excellence*. And as tourists we go to Delphi, not Delphoi. The precisely transliterated form may be pedantically "right," but the pedantry goes against the grain of cultural habit and actual usage.

As a general rule, we have therefore adopted a "mixed" orthography according to the principles suggested above. When a name has been firmly housed in English (admittedly the question of domestication is often moot), the traditional spelling has been kept. Otherwise names have been transliterated. Throughout the series the -os termination of masculine names has been adopted, and Greek diphthongs (as in Iphigeneia) have normally been retained. We cannot expect complete agreement from readers (or from translators, for that matter) about borderline cases. But we want at least to make the operative principle clear: to walk a narrow line between orthographical extremes in the hope of keeping what should not, if possible, be lost; and refreshing, in however tenuous a way, the specific sound and name-boundedness of Greek experience.

2. *Stage directions*

The ancient manuscripts of the Greek plays do not supply stage directions (though the ancient commentators often provide information relevant to staging, delivery, "blocking," etc.). Hence stage directions must be inferred from words and situations and our knowledge of Greek theatrical conventions. At best this is a ticklish and uncertain procedure. But it is surely preferable that good stage directions should be provided by the translator than that the reader should be left to his own devices in visualizing action, gesture, and spectacle. Obviously the directions supplied should be both spare and defensible. Ancient tragedy was austere and "distanced" by means of masks, which means that the reader must not expect the detailed intimacy ("He shrugs and turns wearily away," "She speaks with deliberate slowness, as though to emphasize the point," etc.) which characterizes stage directions in modern naturalistic drama. Because Greek drama is highly rhetorical and stylized, the translator knows that his words must do the real work of inflection and nuance. Therefore every effort has been made to supply the visual and tonal sense required by a given scene and the reader's (or actor's) putative unfamiliarity with the ancient conventions.

3. Numbering of lines

For the convenience of the reader who may wish to check the English against the Greek text or vice versa, the lines have been numbered according to both the Greek text and the translation. The lines of the English translation have been numbered in multiples of ten, and these numbers have been set in the right-hand margin. The (inclusive) Greek numeration will be found bracketed at the top of the page. The reader will doubtless note that in many plays the English lines outnumber the Greek, but he should not therefore conclude that the translator has been unduly prolix. In most cases the reason is simply that the translator has adopted the free-flowing norms of modern Anglo-American prosody, with its brief, breath- and emphasis-determined lines, and its habit of indicating cadence and caesuras by line length and setting rather than by conventional punctuation. Other translators have preferred four-beat or five-beat lines, and in these cases Greek and English numerations will tend to converge.

4. Notes and Glossary

In addition to the Introduction, each play has been supplemented by Notes (identified by the line numbers of the translation) and a Glossary. The Notes are meant to supply information which the translators deem important to the interpretation of a passage; they also afford the translator an opportunity to justify what he has done. The Glossary is intended to spare the reader the trouble of going elsewhere to look up mythical or geographical terms. The entries are not meant to be comprehensive; when a fuller explanation is needed, it will be found in the Notes.

ABOUT THE TRANSLATION

This new tandem-translation of Aeschylus' *Prometheus Bound* combines the vigorous talents of an accomplished young poet with the masterly philology of one of the world's leading Aeschylean scholars.

James Scully in 1967 was awarded the Lamont Poetry Prize by the Academy of American Poets for his first book of verse, *The Marches*. His second book of poetry, *Avenue of the Americas*, was hailed as marking the arrival of a major new poetic talent. The author of two critical works, *Modern Poetics* (1965) and *Modern Poets on Modern Poetry* (1966), Scully teaches English at the University of Connecticut. His collaborator, C. John Herington, is professor of Classics and Talcott Professor of Greek at Yale University. The editor of *The Older Scholia on the Prometheus Bound,* he is also the author of a magisterial monograph, *The Author of the Prometheus Bound* (1970), as well as *Athena Parthenos: A Study in the Religion of Periclean Athens.* He is a frequent contributor of articles, both philological and critical, to professional classical journals, including *Arion,* of which he is a contributing editor.

By old and universal consensus, the *Prometheus Bound* is one of the supreme dramatic achievements of all time. But, strange to say, it has never in the past been translated into poetic English that meets, or even begins to meet, minimal standards of excellence. Admittedly, the obstacles are staggering. Not only has the meaning of the play—and the (lost) trilogy of which it was part—been obscured by imposed ideologies of every stripe, even Aeschylus' authorship has been denied. Dramatically and rhetorically, the demands on the translator are staggering. This, after all, is a play which literally reaches out, with immense metaphysical ambition, for the universe itself; the dramatic "time" of the trilogy extends over millennia and aeons, just as its geography encompasses the world. Across its stage move the great shapes—and the even mightier voices—of Earth, Ocean, Titans, mankind, and the new and terrible lords of Olympos. In its meaning it aims at nothing less than an account, and perhaps a sanction, of human fate as defined in the complex power-politics of an emerging cosmos. And, finally, there is the poetry—the hard, compact, complex, agglutinative Greek of Aeschylus, whose obscure grandeur is periodically shattered by the passionate simplicity of an utterly honest and compassionate human voice.

Formidable demands indeed, requiring apposite skills in the translator. Can it be done? Here, in this new version, we have, I dare to suggest, a translation unique in its uncompromising honesty, in the clarity of its masculine vigor, and its profound interpretive loyalty to the power of the original. The English is fresh, clean, strong; above all, it is *spoken,* with the candor and clarity of real speech, contemporary speech. Direct and eloquent, though there is nothing here for those who prefer their Greek plays to maintain a donnish *dignitas* and *onkos,* a Blimpish "elevation." Ultimately, of course, at peak intensity, Aeschylus may be beyond the power of any living poet to re-create. What matters, I think, is that at long last we should have an English rendering of this play which conveys, unmistakably, to the Greekless reader something of the *grandeur* (no other word will do) and Dionysiac turbulence of this ancient lord of language. But it is my task to present, not to praise. Let the reader judge.

    Lector, intende: laetaberis.

Lincoln, Vermont   WILLIAM ARROWSMITH

CONTENTS

PROMETHEUS BOUND

INTRODUCTION

I THE MYTH

The *Prometheus Bound*, unlike any other extant Greek tragedy, carries us back almost to the beginnings of this universe. It is set in a period when the Olympian Gods were new, and when even the elemental powers of Sea, Earth, and Sky had not yet withdrawn into inert physical matter, but were tangible personalities—loving, begetting, and warring. The great cosmogonic myth to which these monstrous characters belong is older than Greek civilization, and far more widespread. Many elements of it can now be traced in ancient Near Eastern mythology, and some as far afield as ancient Gaul and India.[1] That international dream of our beginnings is in some ways infinitely remote, especially to the imagination of the modern, scientifically educated, reader. Yet its outlines are still worth the effort to grasp, as one approaches the *Prometheus Bound*. For the supreme miracle of the play is perhaps this: out of a far-off creation-story Aeschylus has conjured a political and religious figure whose influence has expanded rather than decreased with the centuries. Today his Prometheus has transported the memories of the myth far beyond its ancient territory—even across the boundaries that have been set up by the ideologies of the twentieth century. Several translations have been published in postrevolutionary Russia, and in 1961 a Chinese translation (with the *Agamemnon*) appeared in the People's Republic of China.

The creation-myth must have been known to Aeschylus in many versions which no longer exist, but luckily we still have the version

1. There is a survey of this question in M. L. West's *Hesiod: Theogony* (Oxford, 1966), which is the standard commented edition of Hesiod's poem. For English translations of this and the other works of Hesiod to be discussed in this section, the reader is referred to *Hesiod, the Homeric Hymns and Homerica*, ed. H. G. Evelyn-White (London and Cambridge, Mass., 1936).

which was probably the most familiar to him and to his intended audience in the middle years of the fifth century B.C. It is embodied in the poems of Hesiod (flourished about 700 B.C.): mostly in his *Theogony*, but also, to some extent, in his *Works and Days*. The *Theogony* teaches how our universe, once it had been formed out of primeval Chaos, fell successively under three régimes, representing three generations of the same divine family. Schematically, and with innumerable figures left out, the family tree given by Hesiod looks like this (the royal consorts in each generation being shown in capital letters):

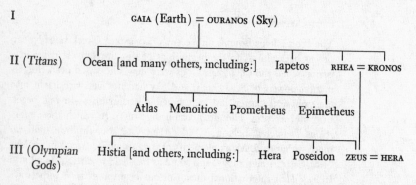

The fates of the three divine governments were varied. Ouranos was castrated by his youngest child Kronos, and dethroned. But Kronos' children were rebellious in their turn. The time came when they revolted under the leadership of the youngest of them, Zeus. They overcame Kronos in a cosmic war, and cast him into the lowest pit of Tartaros, along with most of the other Titans. Since that stupendous upheaval, according to Hesiod, Zeus has reigned in Heaven, secure in his possession of thunder and lightning (*Theogony* 71-72), and attended by his ministers Rivalry, Victory, Power, and Violence (*Theogony* 383-403). Yet two of the older deities managed to survive these heavenly revolutions unharmed: Earth and Ocean. (Ancient myth, for all its strangeness, usually holds fast in its own way to the observable realities. The solid land and heaving waters, as well as the bright, passive sky, couldn't be abolished; they could at best be distanced.) Earth, the aged grandmother of the divine dynasty, lives on throughout Hesiod's story, influencing events by a unique power of her own: *she knows!* She has an awareness of destiny, of the way things really are, that is denied even to the highest male Gods, Ouranos, Kronos, and Zeus himself. Ocean is less important to Hesiod's narrative. He stands somewhat aloof from the politics of the universe, attending conscientiously to his profession, which is to encircle the known world with his massive stream.

Compared to any of these magnificent beings, Hesiod's Prometheus holds a rather insignificant status. He is not at all involved in the great revolution of the Olympians against the Titans. He appears merely as a son of the Titan Iapetos, and he and his three brothers (Atlas, Menoitios, and Epimetheus) are allowed only one, dubious, distinction: all of them sinned against Zeus and failed to get away with it. It is true that Hesiod shows a marked interest in Prometheus' misdeeds and punishment (Theogony 507-616, and again in Works and Days 42-105), but the moral of the story, as he tells it, is, bluntly, that you can't trick Zeus (Theogony 613, Works and Days 105). Prometheus' most notable sin, the theft of fire for mankind, was punished by chaining, and by an eagle which was sent to gnaw his liver; only long afterwards, according to a passage of the Theogony whose genuineness has sometimes been doubted (526-534), did Herakles slay the eagle, "not without the will of Zeus who is Lord on high." Oddly enough, Hesiod's wording does not make it clear whether or not Herakles also released Prometheus. The sin for which Prometheus thus paid so heavily did not even benefit mankind. The gift of fire, which is the only gift that Hesiod mentions, led simply to what (in the eyes of that deplorably antifeminist poet) was unqualified disaster: the first woman, Pandora!

So far as we now know, Prometheus was felt by the Greeks generally—and even, to some extent, by Hesiod himself—as semi-comic: an impudent wag who tempted Providence in unusually ingenious ways, and was properly put down for it. It is a remarkable fact that almost all the ancient Greek literary accounts of Prometheus that survive, whether complete or in fragments, are either overt comedies or at least written in a humorous manner. There was a lost comedy by Aeschylus' Sicilian contemporary, Epicharmus, entitled Prometheus or Pyrrha, and Aristophanes' extant Birds contains an uproarious Prometheus-episode toward its end. As late as the second century A.D. the Greek satirist Lucian is still extracting some tame, civilized fun from Prometheus in his dialogues Prometheus or the Kaukasos and You Are a Verbal Prometheus. Even the great myth of Protagoras about the creation of mankind (as reported in Plato's Protagoras 320c-322d), profoundly serious as its implications are, does not treat Prometheus himself with any great respect, and treats his brother Epimetheus with outright levity. Strangely enough, Aeschylus himself seems originally to have shared the general attitude toward Prometheus. His earliest extant play, the *Persians* of 472 B.C., formed part of a trilogy of tragedies, which was followed, according to the custom at the Dionysiac competitions, by a light-hearted satyr-play. The title of the satyr-play in that production was *Prometheus*, almost certainly with the subtitle *Pyrkaeus* ("the Fire-Lighter"). Not so long ago, a song probably sung by the satyr-chorus in this play came to light on a papyrus. Fragmentary though it is, it allows glimpses of a wild dance, in which the Satyrs caper round "the unwearying glare" of the fire newly given by Prometheus, and praise him for his boon to mankind; they also hope that they'll be joined by a Nymph or two, to complete the pleasure of the occasion.[2] Prometheus was still on Aeschylus' mind—and *still* in a satyric context—in 467 B.C., when he produced his tetralogy on the Theban story (including the extant *Seven Against Thebes*). One of the very few fragments of the satyr-play of that production, the *Sphinx*, mentions Prometheus and his garland—a garland which is "the best of chains."[3] That mysterious garland-chain, as will be seen, recurs later in Aeschylus' work, but then in the altered context of a tragedy. For it seems that very near the end of the poet's life Prometheus began to take on an utterly different shape in his imagination, and to assume, for the first time, the Titanic and tragic stature which is now so familiar to the reader of Goethe, Shelley, or Karl Marx.

II THE PROMETHEUS BOUND

Aeschylus first competed at the Dionysiac festival in or about 500 B.C. During his long career as a playwright he composed, probably, almost ninety tragedies and satyr-plays. Of all that output, only seven tragedies survive complete, dating from the last sixteen years of his life. The *Persians* was produced, as has been mentioned above, in 472 B.C., and the *Seven Against Thebes* in 467. In some subsequent year (there are some grounds for putting it at 463 B.C., but they are not absolutely conclusive), Aeschylus produced the tetralogy whose one surviving play is *Suppliants*. In Spring 458 he pro-

---

2. The fragments of this song are translated by H. Lloyd-Jones in his appendix to H. W. Smyth, *Aeschylus* (London and Cambridge, Mass., 1957), II, p. 566.
3. The fragment is translated in Smyth, *Aeschylus* (see preceding note) II, p. 460.

duced the *Oresteia* tetralogy, of which we have all the tragic plays (*Agamemnon, Choephoroi, Eumenides*), but not the accompanying satyr-play (*Proteus*). Shortly afterwards he left Athens for a voyage to Sicily, from which, as it turned out, he never came back; he died in the Sicilian city of Gela in 456/5 B.C., at the age (probably) of sixty-nine. Unfortunately there exists no direct evidence about the dating of the *Prometheus Bound*. To arrive at a date one's main resource is to compare the play's style, technique, and themes with those of the remaining, dated, plays, but the students who have attempted to apply this method have come to very diverse results. Almost all have agreed that the *Prometheus Bound* cannot be as early as the *Persians*. A minority has even held that it cannot be by Aeschylus at all, but must have been composed at some time after his death. The majority, perhaps, in recent years, has concluded that it must be later than the *Oresteia*, and therefore must date from his last visit to Sicily. The question is not an easy one, and a complete consensus on the answer is hardly to be expected unless some fresh evidence turns up. On the evidence we have, however, the present writer is of the opinion that the last-mentioned conclusion is by far the most likely: the *Prometheus Bound* should belong to the final two years of Aeschylus' life. Most of his reasons are of a technical nature,[4] but one, perhaps, is worth a brief mention here. In the *Suppliants*-tetralogy, and even more in the *Oresteia*, we become aware of two related tendencies in Aeschylus' imagination: a growing preoccupation with the nature of Zeus, and an insistence on the idea of a split between the divine powers of the universe. Neither of these tendencies is visible in the two earliest plays, the *Persians* and the *Seven Against Thebes*; on the other hand, they are brought to a crashing climax in the *Prometheus Bound*, where the human action has become almost insignificant, the split between the divine powers is apparent at the very opening of the play, and the nature of Zeus is questioned as fiercely as it ever was in any ancient pagan work. If this view of the matter is right, then Aeschylus discovered, very late in his life, that the lowly Prometheus who had been on his imagination for at least fourteen years might now be made to serve him in his last and most radical effort to convey his vision of the human and divine state. We shall next try to follow the process of transformation that resulted, so far as the evidence allows.

4. They are presented, with references to differing views on the question, in C. John Herington, *The Author of the Prometheus Bound* (Austin and London, 1970).

In general, the picture of the Universe and of its early history which Aeschylus presupposes in the *Prometheus Bound* is very similar to the picture presented by Hesiod. The significant differences relate to the achievements and genealogy of Prometheus. Aeschylus lays so much emphasis on these differences, especially in the earlier part of the play, that one may well believe that they were strange even to his intended audience; in other words, that at these points he is introducing entirely new material. Thus the first and second episodes (ll. 284-576, and 620-764*) consist largely of straight exposition of the immensely important role which Prometheus has played in divine history and in the civilization of mankind respectively. Such static expository passages, noble poems though they may be in their own right, are rare in Attic drama. Can it be mere coincidence that Hesiod had been completely silent about Prometheus in his roles of cosmic kingmaker and inventor of all human arts? The suspicion grows that in these two episodes Aeschylus is freely inventing —and consequently that the reader here, no less than the original audience, is actually privileged to be in at the creation of that towering Prometheus who has so influenced the modern imagination. Another difference from the Hesiodic tradition, and perhaps the most crucial one of all, is genealogical: Aeschylus makes Prometheus not the grandson of Earth, but her son. The point is emphasized (again, as if it were quite strange to the audience) in lines 311-13. There, and also in lines 35-36 and 1334, Earth is identified, most unusually and no doubt significantly, with the goddess Themis, "Right." In this way Prometheus becomes a member of the older divine generation, the Titans, and uncle to Zeus instead of an obscure cousin. Of his brothers, Aeschylus retains only the spectacular and magnificently suffering figure of Atlas, probably because he felt that the comic, dim-witted Epimetheus and the vague sinner Menoitios were below the dignity of his new Prometheus. A further, and momentous, result of Prometheus' new genealogical position is that in becoming Earth's son he is brought into direct contact with her prophetic powers. He is thus able to share knowledge that is concealed even from Zeus—above all the secret that Zeus, unless warned in time, will some day lie with a girl whose son is fated to be greater than its father. This secret is in fact Prometheus' only weapon in the struggle against Zeus. He naturally will not be heard to name the girl in the course of the *Prometheus Bound*, but from other evidence we

---

* Unless otherwise indicated, line references throughout are to the English translation.

gather that she was the sea-goddess Thetis; and that in the end the Gods judiciously married her off to a mortal, Peleus . . . (The issue of that marriage was Achilles, mightier indeed than his father or any other hero of his time). But in Aeschylus' *Prometheus Bound* all that is in the unborn future. The secret of Thetis' strange destiny is known only to Earth, and to her son Prometheus. Hence, in fact, comes the tension that is built up in the course of the drama. Zeus, who has recently conquered in the war against the Titans, now possesses all the physical power available in the Universe; while Prometheus possesses the knowledge which can, in time, render that power useless and topple Zeus from his throne.

The way is now clear for a consideration of the general structure of the play which Aeschylus proceeded to create. Apart from its tempestuous prologue and finale, there is little physical action. For most of its course the central character, inevitably quite motionless, conducts a series of conversations with a procession of visitors—the Chorus, Ocean, Io, and Hermes—and of these visitors only the Chorus stays for more than a single episode. But before the crude conclusion is drawn (as it often has been) that *nothing happens* between the prologue and the finale, we ought to recall that we are in the presence not of Shakespeare or Webster or Euripides, but of Aeschylus. This is a playwright who, admittedly, rarely does anything twice in the same way; standing as he does so close to that miraculous point in Western history at which *poetry* was transfigured into *drama*, he is freer and less easy to fit into any pattern than most of his successors. But in one respect his method—or is it rather his vision of the way life works?—is consistent. He habitually treats a given physical event as merely the visible manifestation of a vast complex of ideas and moral forces, which sometimes (especially in his later surviving plays) extend to the very boundaries of the Universe. In his best-known play, for instance, the *Agamemnon*, there is far less physical action than in the *Prometheus Bound* itself. Even the single physical event that matters there, the murder of the great king, takes place offstage, and is in a sense thrown out of focus by being seen in detail, by Kassandra, some minutes before it happens. The bulk of the *Agamemnon* explores not that event in itself, but its causes and its significance. Seen from this point of view, the apparently *staccato* episodes of the *Prometheus Bound* present a steady and harmonious progression of ideas. By the end, Prometheus and Zeus and the entire situation within the universe have been transformed: nothing remains in the same state as it was in the noisy and violent prologue, where the silent fire-thief was being passively clamped to the rock for a seemingly limitless and unchangeable punishment. We have already seen how the two episodes following that prologue transform the fire-thief into a cosmic figure. After them, the next great movement of the play is comprised in lines 765-1392. Up to now, Prometheus' knowledge of the Marriage-Secret has been mentioned only with mysterious obscurity (ll. 249-62, 277-83, 743-64); this movement will bring it as far into the open as Prometheus dares, will reveal its central importance, and will also lead directly on to the final catastrophe. The long Io-episode is here framed by two choral odes (765-821 and 1363-92), which are linked thematically, and also musically—the distinctive variety of meter used in the Greek of both odes is particularly striking because it occurs nowhere else in Aeschylus' extant work. The odes both reflect on the irresistible power of the Olympian Gods, on the defenselessness of all lesser beings in the face of it, and on sexual union, which will be the dominating theme of this entire movement. The first ode, however, ends with the solemn, ritual union of Prometheus with his equal Hesione, in marriage, whereas the second dwells on the stark terror of an unequal, violent mating between God and inferior. The long Io-episode which lies between the odes is a specific, and horrible, instance of such divine cruelty. As a result of Zeus' lust, and of the jealousy of Hera, this young mortal girl has been warped in body and mind, and driven from her home to journey in torment. Here the imaginative boundaries of the play suddenly burst outwards from the desolate rock on the Kaukasos range. The accounts of Io's past and future wanderings conduct the hearer in a vast clockwise sweep from her father's palace in Argos, through Prometheus' place of suffering, onwards to the monster-peopled far East, then south to the territory of the Ethiopians, and finally down the Nile, from its fabled source to the Delta. This supreme example of the oppression of humanity by God, expressed in sexual terms, spurs Prometheus to reveal at last the details of the threat that he holds over Zeus. In a dialogue placed at the center of the Io-scene (1138-51), he discloses the secret almost in its entirety, short of giving the name of the girl whom Zeus will choose for his fatal liaison.

The climax of this theme, however, is reserved until immediately after the Io-movement. In a thunderous speech (1393-1425), Prometheus furiously shouts his secret at the sky, in a direct challenge to Zeus. The scene is now set for a second confrontation between Prometheus and the powers of Olympos, of infinitely wider implications than that which took place in the prologue. It is now a war between brute force and unbending knowledge, between the reigning monarch of the Universe and the patron of suffering mankind. The challenge brings Hermes plummeting from heaven, to threaten Prometheus ultimately with Zeus' only available resource—more violence. The Titan still refuses to name the girl, and the play ends in a cosmic storm amid which he sinks into the rock.

The *Prometheus Bound* as a whole thus seems to present a coherent development, even though it is a development of *ideas* rather than of *actions*. In detail there still remain many problematic passages, and we have not yet touched on the most interesting problem of all: the religious and political significance of the story. These questions will be approached in the following section.

III   THE PLAY AND ITS SEQUEL

The long history of the interpretation of the *Prometheus Bound* is almost the history of a mirror. Romantics, liberals, and socialists, gazing into these disturbing depths, have found there an Aeschylean justification of romanticism, liberalism, and socialism, respectively. Authoritarians on the contrary, from the medieval Byzantines onwards, have emphasized with approval the crushing punishment ultimately accorded to the rebel against the Supreme Authority. In a word: *Tell me what you are, and I will tell you what you think of the* Prometheus Bound. . . . The present writer has no reason to believe that he has been specially exempted from this law. The following interpretation is therefore put forward with humility. It is meant not as a definitive pronouncement, but as an indication of some factors which may help the reader to make up his own mind.

We may at least begin with a statement on which, probably, all critics can agree, whatever their ideologies: in the dramatic present of the *Prometheus Bound*, Zeus' government of the universe is represented as a despotism of the most brutal kind. The supreme God is made to look the very pattern of an ancient Greek tyrant (in the most unfavorable sense of that word), and there can be no doubt that this is deliberate. He is given all the stock attributes of the tyrant that are found in Greek historians and political thinkers from Herodotos to Aristotle: he rules without laws (ll. 223, 278), he seduces his female subjects (Io is one example), he plans indiscriminate murder of his people (345), he is so suspicious that he does not even trust his friends (334-36).[5] But the *Prometheus Bound* goes far beyond citing the traditional Greek attributes. Here we reach one of the more uncanny aspects of the play: especially in the prologue and the final scene with Hermes, it presents a study of tyranny *in action*, and its effects on victims and agents alike, which has no parallel at all in ancient literature, and foreshadows the methods of twentieth-century totalitarianism. The following summary of a recent investigation into contemporary brainwashing techniques is worth a few moments' pause: "Isolation, deprivation of sleep, intimidation, endlessly repeated accusations of lying, maintenance of very painful postures, abrupt change of attitude by the interrogator, from vilification to friendly understanding and compassion, and then back again to severity . . . these are basic features. . . . [The prisoner] might have leg chains and manacles applied."[6] Almost every feature of the twentieth-century prison-camp can in fact be paralleled in the *Prometheus Bound*, without pressing the evidence. We see here a political offender whose will must be broken by the régime at all costs, by isolation from all fellow-beings, by torture, by chaining, and even by psychological means (Power's final effort to pervert Prometheus' very name, ll. 130-31, is noteworthy); the too-familiar callous police-agents, Power and his female colleague Violence,[7] who in a modern production might appropriately be clothed in neat black uniforms and jackboots; the gentle, non-political technician, Hephaistos, pressed in to misuse his skill for the régime's infamous purposes; and finally the high-ranking Party official, Hermes, who does not dirty his own hands with violence, but proceeds like an expert brainwasher, alternating between threats and confidential appeals to reason. These parallels between the ancient play and the modern prison seem to confirm the fact that in the *Prometheus Bound* Zeus' régime is being represented as an odious tyranny—not only by the criteria of the ancient Greek city-state, but also by the standards of all democratic societies in all ages.

5. These points are established, with full references to the Greek historians and philosophers, by George Thomson, notably in his edition of the *Prometheus Bound* (Cambridge, 1932), p. 6 ff. Of particular interest is the sketch of a tyrant in Herodotos, *Histories* 3.80, which was written only a decade or two after the presumed date of our play.

6. *Times Literary Supplement*, August 14, 1969, p. 893: from a review of S. M. Meyers and A. D. Biderman (eds.), *Mass Behavior in Battle and Captivity* (Chicago, 1969).

7. The Greek gender of her name indicates almost beyond doubt that Violence is a *female* police-agent.

This factor in the dramatic situation thus seems certain, and it is tempting, with some earlier readers, to come to rest in that sublime and appalling concept: *God is a Tyrant*, bent on suppressing mankind's benefactor, and on preventing the awakening of humanity! But unfortunately, it really is not so simple as that. There are two further factors which seem equally certain, and must equally be taken into account by anybody who wishes honestly to decipher the message of Aeschylus. These factors may be summarized thus:

1. The contradictions in Prometheus as they appear in the extant *Prometheus Bound:*
2. The evidence about the now lost sequels to the extant play— above all, the fragments of the *Prometheus Unbound.*

The contradictions in Prometheus may first be illustrated from his great opening utterance (134-89), which happens to be metrically unparalleled in all Greek drama in that it modulates from speech, to chant, back to speech, to full song, and back to chant, combining, in fact, all the three levels of delivery which were at the disposal of a Greek playwright (these will be further discussed in section IV). Or perhaps "happens" is not the correct word. It may be argued that Aeschylus is deliberately emphasizing at the outset, by musical means, the unparalleled nature of his protagonist. The utterance opens (134-42) with Prometheus' calm, majestic appeal to the elements, which is delivered in unaccompanied speech. Then, very abruptly, Prometheus slips into a chant (143-51) in which he laments his horrible and apparently limitless suffering; but equally abruptly (152) reverts to speech, now asserting that he can foresee every detail of the future, and must endure it. Yet he has already begun again to lament his fate when he is interrupted by the as yet unidentifiable sound and fragrance of the approaching Chorus, which spur him (173) to a burst of full song. At line 181 he reverts to chant, at first proudly defying the Gods, but then again collapsing into sheer panic: "*I'm afraid whatever comes!*." This strange pattern repeats itself in his ensuing lyric dialogue with the Chorus, although it is now no longer accentuated by abrupt changes in the Greek meters. Here his utterances are desperate lamentations, until line 249, where he threateningly mentions the mysterious plan by which Zeus' throne will be endangered. The dialogue closes (277-83) with an even more extraordinary shift of attitude—the vision of a future in which he and Zeus will love one another as friends.

Even on the evidence so far mentioned, Prometheus appears to be deliberately represented as an unstable compound of mortal sufferer and immortal prophet—much as Io, in this same play, is an unstable compound of human and heifer (her heifer-element being expressed most brilliantly, though not solely, in her opening and closing songs). At one moment Prometheus is totally absorbed, as any of us human beings would be, in the emotions and the agonies of the present, while at another he has the limitless and timeless vision of a God. This being so, his moments of inspired prophecy deserve careful inspection by anyone who would understand Aeschylus' total conception of the Prometheus story. They transport us, as they transport Prometheus himself, far away from the hideous dramatic present into a very different future. Most important of all from this point of view is surely Prometheus' culminating prophecy in the Io-scene (1276-1336), which is pointedly prefaced by a convincing proof of his mediumistic powers (1240-75), and concluded by the solemn statement that it is derived from Earth-Themis. In the far future which is opened up by this passage, Zeus does not ultimately lie with Io, but merely restores her to herself and caresses her "with a hand you no longer fear," miraculously begetting a child, Epaphos; from that child descends in turn a long and noble line, culminating in the greatest of all heroes, Herakles; and Herakles frees Prometheus.

Yet in Prometheus' very next speech (1393-1425, following the exit-song of Io and the choral ode), the gentle Zeus, the sane Io, and his own release by Io's descendant have all vanished from his thoughts as if they had never been. Several more such apparent inconsistencies occur in the play; compare the content of lines 143-51 with that of 385-88, 743-64, 1135-37, 1152-55. But Prometheus is inconsistent with himself in other respects also. Although he is a bitter adversary of tyranny and oppression in the dramatic present, he admits to responsibility for the staffwork which resulted in the defeat and imprisonment of Kronos and his fellow-Titans (326-29), to having "helped [Zeus] set up his tyranny" (454-55), and to having organized the power-structure of the victorious régime (625-27). The second of these admissions may have sounded particularly sinister to an Athenian audience, for in the Greek Prometheus uses the same words that are used in the ancient Athenian law directed against anyone who set up, or helped to set up, a tyranny in their city.[8] Equally strange are Prometheus' contradictory attitudes to truth-telling, in the Io scene. At one moment he is promising Io the

8. The law is cited by Aristotle, *Polity of the Athenians*, 16.10.

full, undisguised truth (896-99, 909, 1230-32), at others he is deny-
ing it to her (913, 1157) or masking it in oracular obscurity (1155-
56). Finally, it has recently been shown, with an overwhelming
number of examples, that almost all the odious characteristics attributed to Zeus in this play (mostly by Prometheus)—stubbornness,
anger, rashness, harshness—are also attributed to Prometheus himself by other characters, including sympathizers like the Chorus.[9]

In view of these phenomena, we probably have to recognize that
the *Prometheus Bound*, like the *Agamemnon*, is very far from being
a simplistic opposition between blameless virtue and incurable wick-
edness. Rather we are at a nightmare stage of this universe, in which
the true nature of any character, at any level, is hopelessly elusive. Is
Io a mad heifer or the mother of heroes? Is Prometheus a human
sufferer or a divine seer, a champion of humanity or a discontented
member of the divine totalitarian party? Is Zeus the pitiless dictator
of the universe, or its beneficent father? From the bottom to the
top of the chain of being the ambiguities persist, and there is no
point where the mind can rest in moral or political certainty, with
one possible, mysterious exception: the wisdom and foreknowledge
of Earth. Perhaps the most tormenting ambiguity of all, for those
who have been conditioned to read the *Prometheus Bound* as committed partisans either of Prometheus or of Zeus, will be this: *there
is a strain of Zeus in Prometheus himself.*

Could there, conversely, have been a strain of Prometheus in
Zeus? And could it be that at some time when the universe had
grown older, and the echoes of the terrible convulsions at its beginning had died away, the good qualities in each character, by mutual
attraction, might bring the two together? This is a strange, perhaps
to some even an unwelcome, outcome. Yet it actually seems to be
foreshadowed in one of Prometheus' earlier prophetic moments
(280-83); and once, in the most deliberate of his prophecies, near
the end of the Io scene (1283-89), we glimpse a Zeus who shows a
Promethean gentleness toward a human being. But the testimony of
the *Prometheus Bound* can carry us no farther than that. The moment has arrived when we must look at some other, too often neglected, evidence: the lost play or plays which Aeschylus composed as
an immediate sequel to the *Prometheus Bound*. For if one thing is
absolutely certain, it is that he never meant the extant play to be a

9. This important point was demonstrated by A. J. Podlecki in an article, "Reci-
procity in the *Prometheus Bound*," in *Greek, Roman, and Byzantine Studies*,
vol. 10 (1969), pp. 287-92.

self-contained dramatic unity—that when Prometheus vanishes into the rock at its end we are not witnessing the coda of Aeschylus' symphony, but only the close of a movement. The composition and order of the sequence of Prometheus-plays which Aeschylus originally composed has been very much debated, but the majority of modern students of the subject would probably agree on the following statement.[10] The *Prometheus Bound* was undoubtedly followed immediately by a play entitled *Prometheus Unbound*, of which quite a number of fragments survive. There is some very slight evidence to indicate that the *Unbound* in turn may have been followed by a third play, the *Prometheus Pyrphoros* ("Fire-Carrier") of which there are only three, not very informative, fragments. This sequence presumably constituted a tragic trilogy, to be performed together on one occasion, just like the *Oresteia* (and indeed like the majority of Aeschylus' known productions). It will therefore not have been so much three dramas as a single superdrama falling into three movements, with the action and the ideas developing continuously from the first movement to the last. By all analogies the trilogy should have been concluded by a satyr-play, which would be an independent, semi-comic unit; but if a satyr-play was ever composed for this production, we have no way of identifying it. The tragic trilogy thus reconstructed is often referred to as a whole by modern writers as the *Prometheia*, and this is a convenient, time-saving title—provided one bears in mind that there is no ancient authority for it.

All the fragments of the *Prometheia* that seem to be of the least significance for the understanding of Aeschylus' original design are translated and discussed in the Appendix to the present edition. To our knowledge this is the only such collection of the evidence—including nearly all the ancient allusions to these lost plays, as well as the verbatim quotations from them—available in English translation. The fragments include some wonderful moments of imaginative poetry, but as a whole they are definitely not easy reading. At this point, therefore, we shall merely survey the general conclusions which seem to emerge from them, referring the reader to the Appendix for details.

Above all, the fragments confirm the hypothesis that Prometheus' moments of solemn prophecy in the *Prometheus Bound* are to be accepted as describing what actually happened later in the trilogy. Prometheus was released in the end, and by Herakles, the descend-

10. A discussion of the technical evidence available is given in *The Author of the Prometheus Bound* (above, note 4), Appendix A.

ant of Io. The episode of the Garland (Appendix, fragments 15 through 17), so far as it can now be made out, suggests even that Prometheus' vision (*Bound*, ll. 282-83) of a spontaneous, mutual friendship between himself and Zeus was fulfilled. The general drift of the trilogy now becomes clear, also; it is a universal progress from confusion and torment, at all levels of the universe, toward peace and joy. Phrases of the type "release from sorrows," "freedom from agony," "end of toils" recur like a *leitmotiv* in the extant *Prometheus Bound*; we count twenty-one instances of them in the Greek text, which is only 1093 lines long.[11] Such verbal recurrences on such a scale are unique in Greek tragedy, and we can only account for them as being subliminal preparations of the audience for vast changes that were to take place later in the trilogy. In fact, Prometheus' prophecies in the *Bound* and *Unbound* (to Herakles), as well as the action of the *Unbound* in itself, show that such changes actually occurred. All the major characters—Prometheus himself, Io, and Herakles—seem to have moved on from torment to release. And Zeus? Here we know all too little; but there is some evidence to show that, at least, totally new facets of him moved into the spectator's vision as time progressed. We have already seen how, in the far future, he would cease to lust after Io, or to cause her fear. Further, in fragments 11 and 12 of the *Unbound* Prometheus actually envisages Zeus as *pitying*, an emotion which is utterly alien to Zeus in the *Bound* (1500), being there attributed to Prometheus alone (e.g., 514). It thus seems likely that to the thesis of the *Prometheus Bound*, "Zeus is a Tyrant!", the *Unbound* responded with the antithesis, "Zeus is a Savior!", and that in the light of this response a synthesis became possible: the reconciliation of the almighty power of Zeus with the civilizing intelligence of Prometheus. Many people may find such a development difficult to imagine, in view of the hideous portrait of Zeus that is painted in the *Prometheus Bound*: could the God's reputation ever be salvaged after that? But in fact there is a close parallel to the process in another extant work by Aeschylus, composed near the end of his life. In the first third of the *Eumenides* (part of the *Oresteia*, of 458 B.C.), the Furies are represented as the filthiest of Hell's monsters, hated by the bright Olym-

---

11. In translating, it did not seem possible to give the same literal rendering to each of these phrases each time it occurred, without producing an effect of artificiality. But the *idea* has almost always been kept; examples will be found at l. 151 "end this pain," ll. 396-97 "break free of your agony," ll. 470-71 "find a way free of these agonies," l. 483 "try to have you freed from these agonies."

pian Gods and irreconcilably opposed to their claims. In the middle third this aspect fades out, and we begin to understand them as earth-powers capable of blessing the soil as well as of blasting it. In the finale of the *Eumenides* their beneficent aspect is entirely uppermost, and they are persuaded to join forces with the once-hated Olympians in prospering Athens. Yet if only the first third of the *Eumenides* had survived no student, however adventurous, would have dared to predict that outcome. In the *Eumenides*, as in the whole *Oresteia*, Aeschylus admits no absolutes into this universe until the very end. He is willing to postulate that not merely humanity, but even the Gods, even the supreme God himself, are ambiguous, many-sided phenomena, good and evil; and that only time will painfully uncover the good in any of them, making possible a harmonious world. The appalling realism of the first half of this postulate, and the soaring optimism of the second, are neither of them easy to grasp in this age of gray ideologies. Yet it may, possibly, be one clue to the *Prometheia*.

Even if this parallel holds good, however, we still have to confess defeat on most fronts. The story told in the entire trilogy as Aeschylus conceived it, its mechanisms, and the motivations of its participants, remain beyond us. The negligence of ancient scribes (or was it just the quiet, aimless work of mice or moths in some Byzantine library?) has deprived us of two-thirds of the poet's design; and in so doing has carried away much of the evidence for the interpretation even of the extant one-third, the *Prometheus Bound*. It is difficult to make up one's mind whether, in the long run, this loss has harmed or profited the imagination of mankind. We may well have been denied one of the most magnificent political and religious dramas ever composed in the Western world, and yet, and yet . . . the solitary play which survives has generated new poems and new theories in cultures and languages that Aeschylus never knew. Perhaps the greatest reward of a reading of the *Prometheus Bound* in any century since the fall of Rome has been that the reader has been forced by it to construct for *himself* some response to the play's fearsome thesis on humanity, God, and government. So, where the ancient poem now abandons him, only one-third of the way through its course, an eternally modern poem begins: his own.

IV   STAGING AND STAGE-DIRECTIONS

In the matter of staging, as in almost every other, the *Prometheus Bound* presents special problems. There is no reliable information about the way it was first performed—nor indeed about when or where the performance took place. If we are right in dating the play to the very end of Aeschylus' life, during his residence in Sicily, then the poet did not live to see it staged in his own city. On the other hand, the parodies in Aristophanes (especially at the end of the *Birds*, of 414 B.C.) leave little doubt that by this comedian's time the *Prometheus* had been performed before Athenian audiences. We know, in fact, that Aeschylus' son Euphorion later produced a number of his father's unpublished tragedies (presumably found among his papers after his death in Gela), and won four victories with them in the Dionysiac competitions. The *Prometheus* and its trilogy could well have been among these. As a setting, then, for the first production, it is reasonable to envisage the Theater of Dionysos at Athens. There will be a *skēnē* or background-building with two projecting side-wings, an actor-area in the long narrow rectangular space extending between those wings, and a round dancing-floor for the Chorus in front of the actor-area. For specific information about the staging of the *Prometheus*, our first recourse must be—as usual—to the Greek text itself. From this one can deduce with almost complete precision (a) the points where characters enter and exit and (b) the manner in which each part of the play was delivered. Item (b) may require some explanation. There were three types of delivery in the Athenian theater, each traditionally associated with its own meter or meters. Since the meter is, of course, still preserved in the Greek verses, we can in almost all cases state how any given section was uttered. The Greek tragedian had at his disposal: (1) *unaccompanied speech*, associated with the six-foot iambic line which is the almost universal dialogue-meter in Greek drama. (2) A delivery known in Greek as *parakatalogē*, which was accompanied instrumentally, and was something midway between speech and melodic song, like our modern recitative; it was mostly associated with the rapid-moving anapestic meter. In our stage-directions this kind of delivery is referred to as *chant*. In the *Prometheus* its use nearly always indicates rising emotions, quickening tempo; a good example is in the finale (1593-end), where it marks the coming of the great storm. (3) Fully melodic *song*, instrumentally accompanied, and associated with an almost endless variety of lyric rhythms. There can be great fascination in following Aeschylus' handling of these three types of delivery for dramatic purposes. Here, long after every ancient lyre has been broken and nearly every written note lost, there is still some possibility of appreciating him in his aspect of operatic musician, and a virtuoso at that. There are even passages, above all

the opening speech of Prometheus which was analyzed above, where
an understanding of the variations in delivery seems almost essential to an understanding of Aeschylus' meaning.

A few further indications about the staging can be extracted from
the Greek text. The mask of Power seems to have been hideously
ugly (line 120). The mask of Io was crowned, grotesquely, with
heifer-horns (1002-3). Ocean somehow appeared mounted on a
monster which was winged, and yet had four legs (433, 572-74). Beyond this, all is uncertain. In the ancient Greek commentary on
Aeschylus' seven plays preserved in our oldest surviving manuscript
(the venerable "Medicean manuscript" in the Laurentian Library,
Florence), there are a few notes referring to the staging of the
Prometheus Bound. They run as follows:

On line 190 (opening words of the Chorus): "They utter these words
while being swung in the air by means of a mēchanē [crane]; for it would
be absurd that they should converse from below with Prometheus, who
is high up. But while he is talking to Ocean [i.e., in the scene 431 ff.],
they come down to the ground."

On line 431 (opening words of Ocean): "The arrival of Ocean provides
the Chorus with a suitable opportunity to get down from the mēchanē.
. . . Ocean is riding on a four-legged griffin."

On line 577: "The Chorus, having come down to the ground, sings the
stasimon [ode]."

The authorship and date of these notes are unknown; at most we can
say that they can hardly have been compiled less than two centuries
after Aeschylus' death, and that they may be several centuries later
still. One is at liberty, if one will, to assume that they may preserve
genuine information about the original production of the Prometheus, or at least of some production in classical times, and quite
a number of students have done so. In that case Prometheus will
somehow be elevated high above the stage, and the entire Chorus
(numbering twelve or fifteen) will be swung in on a crane and will
hover around him until Ocean enters, when they will descend to
stage-level and disembark. But we confess that our imaginations bog-
gle at the implied spectacle, and we prefer to believe that the flight
and descent of the Chorus were represented simply by mime (see,
further, our note on ll. 190-283). On the other hand, the ancient
commentator's assertion that Ocean and his monster were brought
in on a crane seems acceptable. Indeed, it is hard to imagine any

other way of doing it; and there are many parallels in fifth-century drama (even as early as the lost *Psychostasia* of Aeschylus himself) for the introduction of a winged character, or a character on a winged mount, by such mechanical means.

The reader now has before him such meager ancient evidence as exists concerning the staging of the *Prometheus*. The stage-directions which we have inserted in the present edition are mostly inferences from the text itself; one or two depend on the ancient notes which have just been described; here and there we have added our own brief hints as to staging or delivery. But the reader is urged to bear in mind that none of these directions derives from Aeschylus himself, and to exercise his own judgment accordingly.

The question of physical staging is, of course, one thing, while the fantastic scene conjured in the imagination by Aeschylus' verse is quite another. The latter could never be reproduced in its fullness on any stage, whether ancient or modern (film, unfortunately, has never yet been properly exploited as a medium for Aeschylean drama). The imagined setting lies where, for Aeschylus, the world ends—the Kaukasos range, probably thought of as extending between the further end of the Black Sea and the encircling Ocean.[12] Across some chasm high in those desolate mountains, Prometheus is fettered. Far below he can glimpse the endless glitter of the waves (l. 137); and somewhere down there, within earshot of the tremendous clang of Hephaistos' sledge, are the sea-caverns where Ocean and his daughters dwell (193-97, 444-47). Thus the setting remains until the great storm at the end, which, again, must always have been realized for audiences primarily by the magic of Aeschylus' verse. The ancient theater had its primitive thunder-machines, and the modern producer might make effective use of drums here; but neither will carry one far, in comparison with the words. In this final upheaval of the elements Prometheus will be swallowed by the mountain chasm, as Hermes has threatened (ll. 1551-55). What becomes of the Chorus is not clearly indicated in Aeschylus' text, but we prefer to imagine that they disappear—also swallowed up by the collapsing rocks—somewhat before Prometheus' last terrible appeal to the elements. "Everyone else having left, Prometheus speaks his words to the bright sky [aithēr], just as he did in the beginning," was the guess of one of the greatest of medieval Byzantine scholars,

12. The Caspian Sea was not generally known to be an inland sea until the time of Alexander the Great, more than a century after Aeschylus' death.

Demetrios Triklinios, in his commentary on lines 1661-63. It is only a guess (Demetrios probably had no more reliable information than we do on such points) but it makes sense. Prometheus' last words, like his first, will thus be spoken in utter loneliness—except for the eternal, mysterious presence of the elements.

New Haven   C.J.H.
July 1974

A NOTE ON THIS TRANSLATION

Any language is a unique complex of cultural associations, so we have tried to translate not only the words but the realities they are charged with. That is, this translation starts from commonplace assumptions and intentions. Nonetheless it has turned out to be more idiomatic, yet also more literal, than other versions of the play. We have been somewhat literal in our handling of metaphor. Wherever possible, Aeschylus' 'metaphors'—which are not metaphors, strictly speaking, but the images generated by his unabstracted apprehension of the world—have been kept more or less intact. For instance, l. 646 is usually rendered as "houses made of bricks," whereas here it is "brick-knitted houses" ("brick-woven" would be the literal translation, but "woven" is so overused as a metaphor that it seems inert, no longer image-able). We have held to this and other images not merely because they are there, though that might be reason enough, but because they are startlingly right and precise. In its context, the image of "brick-knitted houses" does more than note the cultural advance signalled by the move from caves into houses. It evokes a profound technical breakthrough: the discovery that bricks might be made and built with . . . if, instead of being heaped or stacked atop one another, they were overlapped or staggered. Aeschylus' phrase, which also suggests the texture of brick, is a fresh realization of something that almost anyone else would have taken for granted. The realization is condensed, fleeting, but it is there and ought to be preserved. It has something to tell us.

To keep faith with the spirit of the Greek text, we have at times had to reach through its 'letter' so as to draw submerged metaphors nearer the surface. Io characterizes Argos as being "unmixed in his rage." Those are her actual words. Here, however, those words are translated as "his rage the rage/of raw wine" (ll. 1010-11), for the simple reason that a word-for-word translation would have given little clue as to their significance, their cultural ambience. In fact the original phrase conceals a wine metaphor. The Greeks believed that the drinking of unmixed wine, wine undiluted by water, drove men crazy. Argos' rage, then, was unadulterated and therefore mad, barbarous.

This translation also tries to be idiomatic: partly to convey the familiarity of concepts that really are familiar, but which seem remote when couched in translatese; and partly to simplify. Aeschylus' text suffers no serious distortion if "we come in winged rivalry of speed" or "in swift rivalry of wings" is rendered as "we raced ourselves here" (l. 192), especially as the "wings" in the Greek are probably no more than a stage direction, a notation on the costume of the Chorus. Mostly, however, idiomatic speech has been used to take graphic but alien images and, without rubbing off all their strangeness, make them accessible. At one point, one point only, we have dovetailed a literal and an idiomatic translation of a single line. The Greek: "Who, then, is the helm-swinger of Necessity?" And the English translation: "But who swings the helm?/who brings Necessity about?" (ll. 751-2). By observing the second part of that line, which contains a nautical metaphor that has been worn down into idiomatic usage, one may have some sense of the transformations that have occurred between the original text and its translation. We have, then, tried to render the play idiomatically without, in the process, domesticating it. Aeschylus' audacity and 'otherness' should come through untamed. He is not, and should not seem to be, our contemporary. Immediately present, yes. But as himself, not quite as one of us.

As we note in the introduction, verse distinctions among speech, chant and song are essential dramatic properties of the play. Naturally we have tried to maintain those distinctions. Although it should be noted that possibly the least Aeschylean aspect of this translation is in the speech rhythms. These rhythms, as the narrative manners of Prometheus himself, start from one basic assumption: that their function is not merely to convey certain information, but to communicate the experience of that information. Which is what Prometheus does with kennings. For example, his "seawandering/ linen wingd/chariots for sailors" (ll. 677-79) forces us to reimagine ships, to encounter them as a marvellous, primitive invention before it has evolved its own proper name. So, too, the delayed timing of Prometheus's descriptions: "And their three sisters live nearby:/ repulsive with hair/not hair, they're wingd/snake wool! it's/GOR-GONS!" (ll. 1196-1200). Once a thing is 'named,' its mystery and spring and terror are muted, locked up. But here as elsewhere, Prometheus witholds the domesticating name until the last possible moment. Truly to know what "Gorgons" are, one has to sweat out the disorienting, by turns dawning and erupting, realization of them. In this translation we have attempted through our rhythms to keep touch with this nervous, muscular, sensuous process. At some level it seems to bear not only on the rhetorical devices of Prometheus, but on the sensibility of Aeschylus as well.

This is one play that seems to have been written with the head, hands and heart: bunched, impacted, in the solar plexus. Ideally it would not be read or seen, but undergone. Of course the translation does not pretend to approach the standards suggested here; it attempts, simply, to acknowledge them.

Storrs   J.S.
September 1974

PROMETHEUS BOUND

CHARACTERS

POWER   male, an agent of Zeus
VIOLENCE   female, an agent of Zeus
HEPHAISTOS   blacksmith, fire worker, god of craftsmanship
PROMETHEUS
CHORUS   the daughters of Ocean
OCEAN   old god of the world's waters
IO   the heifer girl
HERMES   the messenger god

PROMETHEUS *is dragged by* POWER *and* VIOLENCE; HEPHAISTOS, *lugging chains and blacksmith tools, trails after them.*

POWER And so we've come to the end of the world.
To Scythia: this howling waste
                              no one passes through.

Hephaistos, now it's up to you.
What the Father wants done
      you've got to do.
On these overhanging cliffs
      with your own shatter-proof irons
you're commanded:
Clamp this troublemaking bastard to the rock.   10

After all, Hephaistos, it was your glowing flower
      FIRE
      —the power behind all
            works of hands—
he stole it, he gave it away
to human beings.
That's his crime, and the Gods demand
      he pay for it.
He must submit
      to the tyranny of Zeus   20
and like it, too.
He'll learn.

He's got to give up
feeling for humanity.

HEPHAISTOS Power and Violence . . . you've already carried out
      your orders from Zeus,
you're free to go now.
But me, I haven't the heart to chain this god
      this brother!

to this stormbeaten ravine.   30
         And yet I must.
   It's heavy business
to shrug off the Father's word . . .

Prometheus, I know you for what you are:
the headlong, steep thinking son
      of Themis: your levelheaded mother.
Yet against my will, as against yours
I'll spike you to this
    inhuman cliff.
Nobody's here, no human voice   40
will come through to you.
When the bloom on your cheek is burnt
    black by the sun
you'll be glad when night with her veils of starcloud
covers up the glare,
And again glad when at dawn, the sun
      scatters the hoarfrost off.
But always you'll be crushed by the load
    of each, every moment.
The one who will set you free   50
hasn't even been born.

This is what you get
for loving humankind.

You, a god, outraged the Gods.
Weren't you afraid?
You gave mere people
what people should not have
   Prometheus!
Now you must stand watch
over this brute rock   60
and never bend your knee,
you won't sleep, won't move,
no you'll
    sigh and howl

and won't be heard. No

Zeus is not
    about to mellow.
Every ruler who's new
is hard.

POWER MOVE damn it! What good's your pity?   70
    Why don't you hate the god
        the Gods hate?
    Didn't he betray you? He gave humans a power
    meant for you!

HEPHAISTOS We're family, we're friends: there's power in that, too.

POWER Sure. But how can you refuse the Father's
        orders!
    Don't they scare you even more?

HEPHAISTOS (groaning)
    You are pitiless . . . shameless too. You always were.

POWER No use whining about it. He's had it.   80
    Don't work yourself up
           over a lost cause.

HEPHAISTOS It's this work, these masterful hands of mine—
    that's what I hate!

POWER What for? Fact is, the craft you work at
    wasn't to blame for this.

HEPHAISTOS Still, I wish it had fallen to someone else.

POWER Every job's a pain, except
        for the God at the top.
    Only Zeus is free.   90

HEPHAISTOS (*gesturing toward* PROMETHEUS)
Obviously. What can I say.

POWER THEN GET A MOVE ON! Throw the chains on him—
before Zeus sees you loafing on the job.

HEPHAISTOS Look here, the iron's at hand. You aren't blind.

POWER Clamp his wrists, real hard. Now the sledge: with all
your might, quick, spike him to the rock!

HEPHAISTOS OK OK I'm doing my job. I'm doing it right.

POWER Strike! Strike! Harder. Squeeze. He's too shrewd:
where there's no way out, still, he'll find one.

HEPHAISTOS Well, here's one arm he'll never work free.   100

POWER Then spike the other, hard. He's got to learn:
'intellectual' that he is, next to Zeus he's stupid.

HEPHAISTOS No one can say I didn't do
                    justice to this job!
Except Prometheus.

POWER Now the arrogant jawbone, of *wedge*: batter
it hard, you, crunch through his chest!

HEPHAISTOS (*cries out: striking, recoiling*)
PROMETHEUS! it's your agony I cry for!

POWER You shying off again? Moaning over enemies of Zeus?
Watch out, or you'll be moaning for yourself.   110

HEPHAISTOS You see something no one should see.

POWER I see this bastard getting what he deserves.
Now! Slap those iron bands around his ribs.

HEPHAISTOS I do what I have to do. Don't push it.

POWER I'll push you alright! the way a hunter sics his dogs.
Now get under. Shackle those legs.

HEPHAISTOS (*having gotten under, getting hastily back up*)
There, the job's done. I've made short painless work of it.

POWER Now, hard as you can, hammer the shackles INTO him!
Watch it now. The Boss checks everything out.

HEPHAISTOS I can't tell which is worse: your looks or your loud mouth.   120

POWER So be a bleeding heart! Me, I'm thick-skinned,
but don't blame me for that. I am what I am.

HEPHAISTOS Let's get out of here. He's ironbound, hand and foot.

(HEPHAISTOS *hobbles off.*)

POWER (*finally addressing* PROMETHEUS)
You cocky bastard: now steal
        powers from the Gods.
And for what?
            Things that live and die!
Tell me sir, can humanity drain off
        a single drop of your agony?
The Gods called you "Resourceful,"   130
        that's a rich one.
You'll need resources, to squirm out of this
first-rate ironwork.

(POWER *strides away. After a moment* VIOLENCE *follows
him, silent as ever.*)

PROMETHEUS (*alone: speaking, invoking*)
Light, light, you
        bright sky, winds on the wing, you rivers
            springing up, and you

33

the waves the immense laughter easing the sea—
            now
Earth, mother of us all
            and you, Sun, watching over all: 140
            see
what a god can suffer at the hands of the Gods!

(*chanting*)
            These are the tortures
            I must struggle with: through ten thousand years
            of flesh raked away.

            This new Dictator
            of the Fortunate . . . *He* had these chains made
            to put me to shame!

            This agony I
            feel, I feel it coming too! At what point   150
            will He end this pain?

(*speaking*)
Wait, what am I saying?
I know how it all turns out:
            no unforeseen
heartbreaks for me.
            I see,
I do what I'm bound to do, and take the consequence
            as best I can.
I know: no one
wrestles Necessity down.   160

Yet it's hard to speak, and just as hard
not to speak, of what has happened . . .

For the power, the glory I gave to human beings
            I'm bound in irons.
I tracked down fire, where it springs from.
And stole it. I hid
            the spark in a fennel stalk, and brought it

to human beings. Now it shines
    forth: a teacher
showing all mankind the way to all the arts there are.   170
That's my crime. That's why
I'm hammered in chains under the open sky.

              (*A distant throbbing arises, approaches:* PROMETHEUS
                                        bursts into song.)
              But what's that sound, that perfume? I can't see
                        what flies at me!
                        Is it a God
              or is it human, or a mingling of the two,
                        who comes to this rock
                        at the edge of the world?

(*breaking off*)
To make a show of me? Or what?
Then look! At a god savaged by irons   180

(*chanting*)
              an enemy of Zeus

        hated by all those Gods
        who strut through His vestibule,

        hated because I love
        mankind more than I should.

        Still it comes! But what?

        Light air whispers
        fluttering with wings!

        I'm afraid whatever comes!

              (DAUGHTERS OF OCEAN, *a chorus of barefoot girls
              with the wings of sea birds, flock breathlessly in.*)

CHORUS (*dancing, singing*)
>> Don't be afraid: we came   190
>> because we love you.
>> We raced ourselves here.
>>
>> Old Father Ocean
>> groaned, but let us go.
>> High winds lofted us here.
>>
>> The pounding irons rang
>> right through our cave.
>> We were beside ourselves!
>>
>> We forgot to be shy: look
>> we come barefoot.   200
>> Our wings hurried us here.

PROMETHEUS (*chanting*)
>> Ah, children of Tethys
>> mother of so many others!
>> You're your father's daughters
>> too, I see—
>> old Ocean
>> who never sleeps, but streams
>> coiling around the world!
>>
>> . . . Look! Look at me.
>> Chained in the rockpeaks   210
>> of this ravine,
>> I'll stand a watch
>> no one envies me.

CHORUS (*dancing, singing*)
>> Prometheus, I see
>> but through a mist of fear.
>> Tears darken my eyes.
>>
>> I see, I see your body
>> withering on this rock,
>> racked by unspeakable irons.

New masters sail Olympus.   220
   Look now, how Zeus lords it!
His rules are new, they're raw.

He rules beyond the law.
   Giant Things that used to be
He wipes out completely.

PROMETHEUS (*chanting*)
   He should have buried me
   under this earth, and under
   Hades, cave of the dead,
   down bottomless Tartaros.
   With breakproof chains, with torture   230

   still, that would be better.
   No God there, no no one
   could make a fool of me.
   But here, while I hang
   the winds toy with me

   I writhe, my enemies smile.

CHORUS (*dancing, singing*)
      What brute hearted God
        would smile at this?
      Who wouldn't howl feeling with you   240
        at this outrage?
      None but Zeus. His spite, His will
        won't bend: but crush
      the children of Father Sky.
        Zeus won't let up
      till Zeus has had enough

      unless, against all odds, He's over-
      thrown by ambush! Done with!

PROMETHEUS (*chanting*)
   My day will come: though this

Commander of the Fortunate
tortures me, chains me up,   250
yet still my day will come.
He'll need me, to tell Him how
a new conspiracy
(I see it even now)
strips Him of His scepter
and all His privileges.

He'll never mystify me,
not with honey tongued charms
singing, to draw me out.
Never, I'll never cringe   260
to tell these things, despite
His lead heavy threats.

Not till He breaks these chains.

Not till He pays me all
He owes for this outrage.

CHORUS (*dancing, singing*)
You're brave, you won't
give in to pain.
And yet, your speech is much too free.
Fear quick fear
pierces our fluttering hearts: 270
whatever must become of you
on this sea of pain,
and when will you
arrive, safe on the shore?

Your words can't touch, your words won't move
the brute heart of Kronos' Son.

PROMETHEUS (*chanting*)
He's savage, I know. He keeps
justice in His fist.
But with this hammer blow

He'll soften, He'll calm down   280
His blind stubborn rage.

He'll come to me, as a friend,
I'll love my friend again.

(*The music ends:* PROMETHEUS *and the* CHORUS *speak
                                   without accompaniment.*)

CHORUS   O tell us, tell us everything!
Having arrested you,
on what charge does Zeus
torture, humiliate you?
Tell us the whole story, please
. . . but only
if it doesn't hurt to tell.   290

PROMETHEUS   It's painful to speak, it's painful
not to.
Every way, there's misery.

As soon as the Gods broke into factions
civil war was breaking out.
Some wanted to unseat
old Kronos.
Imagine! they wanted Zeus to rule.
Others though were deadset against it,
against Zeus   300
lording it over them.
Bringing good advice then, I went to the Titans
—the sons of Father Sky
and Mother Earth—
and went for nothing.
They brushed off
my sophisticated stratagems.
By sheer willpower and brute force
they dreamed
they would win with ease.   310

My mother Themis, who is also called Earth
    (she's one, only one, always the same form
        though she has many names)
she had sung time and again
the way the future goes:
how the war is won
    not by brute force
but by cunning, as fate would have it.
Yet even while I spelled this out for them
they wouldn't so much as look at me.   320
What could I do?
As things stood then, it seemed best
    to take my mother, and together
      we went as volunteers
                into the open arms of Zeus.
Thanks to the strategy I devised
the black hole of Tartaros holds and hides
    archaic Kronos
and all his allies too.
This Tyrant of the Gods   330
    so profited from my help
He paid me back in full,
with evil.
      Because all tyranny
is infected with this disease:
it never trusts its friends.

But you asked why He tortures me.
Listen. I'll make it clear . . .

The war's no sooner over
    than there He is, on His father's throne,   340
dealing out privileges to the different Gods.
And so, He makes a hierarchy of powers.
But for the suffering race of humankind
    He cared nothing,
He planned to wipe out the whole species
and breed another, a new one.

And no one dared stand up against this thing
    but me!
I alone had the courage.
I saved humanity from going down   350
    smashed to bits
into the cave of death.
       For this
I'm wrencht by torture:
    painful to suffer,
       pitiable to see.
I began by pitying people (things that die!)
    more than myself, but for myself
I wasn't thought fit to be pitied.
Instead, I'm brought to order   360
    without mercy—
a sight to bring
disgrace on the name of Zeus.

CHORUS   What iron heart what breast hacked out of rock
would not howl
    feeling with you
       Prometheus!
I would not have wished to see this
yet now I *do* see, I'm   370
heartstruck.

PROMETHEUS   Yes, this is a pitiful sight . . . to my friends.

CHORUS   You didn't, perhaps, go beyond what you've told us?

PROMETHEUS   Humans used to foresee their own deaths. I ended that.

CHORUS   What cure did you find for such a disease?

PROMETHEUS   Blind hopes. I sent blind hopes to settle their hearts.

CHORUS   What a wonderful gift you helped mankind with!

PROMETHEUS   What's more, I gave them fire.

CHORUS   Flare-eyed fire!?
Now! In the hands of these
            things that live and die!?   380

PROMETHEUS Yes, and from it they'll learn many skills.

CHORUS So these are the charges on which Zeus

PROMETHEUS   TORTURES ME
and in no way eases these agonies!

CHORUS But isn't there a fixed point at which
            your agony must end?

PROMETHEUS None. It will end
            only when HE sees fit.

CHORUS When He sees fit! What hope is that?
Don't you see,   390
            you went wrong!
But then, it gives me no pleasure to tell you
            how you went wrong,
besides it's painful for you to hear.
So, enough of that.
You must find a way to break
free of your agony.

PROMETHEUS It's easy enough for the bystander,
            who's not bogged down in sorrow,
to advise and warn   400
the one who suffers.

Myself, I knew all this
and knew it all along.
Still,
      I *meant* to be wrong.
I knew what I was doing.
Helping humankind
      I helped myself to misery

And yet I never dreamed it would be like this,
　　　this wasting away against the air hung cliffs   410
　　the desolate mountain top
　　　　the loneliness
So don't now, don't
　　　cry over this, the sorrow that is.
But come down to earth.
Hear what's to come, hear the story to its end.

Obey me, obey!
Bear with me
　　　now it's my turn for misery.
Sorrow wanders about the world   420
touching on each of us, and each in turn.

CHORUS (*wheeling deeper into the ravine, nearer* PROMETHEUS:
　　　chanting in gusts)
　　　　　　　　　　　Prometheus
　　　　　　　　we come and gladly,
　　　　　　　glad you called to us.
　　　　　　Out of the pure clean air
　　　　　　　O air currents
　　　　　　　　the birds ride
　　　　　I come, coming to set my light
　　　　　　foot on this harsh rock,
　　　I'll hear out your sorrows to the end.   430

(*suddenly a birdhorse billows down with an overwhelming
　　　　　　　　rider on its back: this is* OCEAN)

OCEAN (*chanting*)
　　　　　At this point my long journey ends, Prometheus,
　　　　　because here you are. Didn't use the reins, either,
　　　　　I just steered this wingéd monster by sheer willpower.
　　　　　But you may rest assured, my *heart* goes out to you—
　　　　　it couldn't do otherwise, seeing that we're kin,
　　　　　and even if we weren't, it would: for there's no one,
　　　　　no one I respect more than you. You can believe that.

I haven't it in me to go around mouthing
highsounding hollow words. Look I'll prove it: tell me
what I can do for you . . . and then you'll never say   440
you have a steadier friend than your friend Ocean!

PROMETHEUS What's this! Have you too come
              to witness my pain?
          How did you dare abandon
                  the great stream that bears your name
                      and the rock arches of the sea caves
                          the sea itself has made—
          to come to this, this
          motherland of iron!
          And why? To see what's happened to me?   450
              To howl feeling with me?
          Well here's a show for you: look at this
                  friend of Zeus!
          I helped Him
              set up His tyranny,
          now I'm wrencht with torture
          ordered by Him.

OCEAN I do see, Prometheus. And what I wish to give you
              (smart as you are)
          is the best advice of all: 460
                          Know thyself.
          Also, rehabilitate yourself.
          The Gods have a new Tyrant,
              follow the new line!
          If you throw such sharp words around
          why even Zeus, even though He's seated way up there,
                  may hear!
          Then agonies that crowd you now
          will seem like child's play.
          You're suffering: calm down, find a way   470
              free of these agonies.
          This may sound old-fashioned, but
          The braggart gets more than he bargained for.

You don't keep your profile
   low enough, you don't
   give in to torture: you insist
    on more of the same!
Let me be your teacher, and you won't
    stick your neck out,
not when there's a hard Chief-of-State   480
in power, accountable to no one.

I'll go now, and try to have you
   freed from these agonies.
Meanwhile keep quiet, don't run off at the mouth.
Clever as you are, you should know by now
To a loose tongue, punishment comes.

PROMETHEUS (ironically)
      How I envy you:
having been such a great help in my struggle
    you're beyond blame!
Now too, leave me alone, forget it.   490
You won't ever change His mind, it's set.
You look out for yourself, you're headed for trouble.

OCEAN You give advice better than you take it,
look at you!
      I'm going now, don't try to haul me back.
I'm confident, absolutely confident
Zeus will grant what I ask:
to free you from these agonies.

PROMETHEUS One thing I admire in you, and always will:
you're not at a loss for good intentions.   500
But don't bother,
    it's useless to bother on my account
    . . . that is, if you really intend to.
No, keep quiet, stay out of this.
I've my misfortune, but that's no reason for me to wish
   as many as possible should suffer too,

not when I'm already
    torn by the anguish
of Atlas, my brother:
                     who stands where evening is,   510
    pressing his shoulder to the unbearable
        pillar that holds
the sky from the earth!

Pity cut me to the quick, too, when I saw
    that child of Earth,
the hotblooded monster of the Cilician caves,
       Typhon
    with his hundred flickering heads
as he, too, was overpowered by violence.
He stood up against all the Gods: 520
      terror
    hissed through his horrible jaws, his eyes
glared, a lightningd
  DEATH'S HEAD!
As though he'd explode the tyranny of Zeus
by violence!
But then on *him*
     Zeus drove the sleepless thunderbolt,
    plunged the fire spurting shaft
down, it slammed   530
the loud bragging pride out of Typhon—
    struck through, scorcht
      his heart out, it
thundered his strength away.
Now that helpless sprawl of a body lies
    near the sea narrows,
clenched by the massive roots of Etna,
    while at the summit
Hephaistos sits, pounding the glowing mass of iron.
     One day in time to come   540
fire rivers will gush up: white hot fangs will gouge
the smooth, fruitful fields of Sicilý!
That will be Typhon
    fuming:

though Zeus's lightning bolt has burnt him out, still
     he'll boil up, he'll jet
fountains of rage and fire.

But you've been around, you don't need me
to teach you this.
Save yourself any way you can.   550
I have, now, my own misfortune: which I'll bail to the dregs
     until the wrathful mind
       of Zeus . . . lets up.

OCEAN   Don't you know, Prometheus:
a sick mind may be cured by words.

PROMETHEUS Yes, if the time's right. But when that mind is still
infected with rage, you can't force the swelling down.

OCEAN All right then, teach me this: what's the harm
if daring is mixed with good intentions?

PROMETHEUS Useless makework! simplistic innocence!   560

OCEAN Then let me suffer such disease.
When one is wise, it's wisest to seem foolish.

PROMETHEUS As will be seen: that's my condition, not yours.

OCEAN Your drift is obvious: you want to send me home.

PROMETHEUS Yes. If you feel sorry for me, you'll get yourself hated

OCEAN by Him? the One newly seated on the Throne of Power!

PROMETHEUS Yes. Watch out, or His heart may turn angry on you.

OCEAN I learn that, Prometheus, just by looking at you.

PROMETHEUS LEAVE! GET GOING! NOW YOU'VE GOT THE
                POINT, KEEP IT IN MIND!

OCEAN Before the words are out of your mouth
                    I'm going!
            My four-legged bird
                    strokes the smooth
            skyways with his wings.
            For sure: he'll be glad to bed down
            at home, in his own stall.

                (OCEAN *and his monster swing upward, and away.*)

CHORUS (*dancing and singing an ode*)
                        Prometheus, your savage fate
                            has made me cry.
                        My cheeks are wet
                    with tears welling from my delicate eyes   580
                        as river water, or the falling dew.
                    It's horrible: Zeus dictates with laws
                            He made Himself,
                    He bares the spearpoint of His pride, over
                        the Gods that used to be.

                The whole earth now howls with grief:
                        everything mourns
                        the bold, emblazoned
                glowing ancient glory that used to be
        and be yours and your family's, before this grief.   590
                    And those peoples who have set
                        their roots in the plains
                        near Asia's holy ground,
                        they feel your howling pain

                    as do the girls of Colchis
                who never tremble in battle;
                and, too, the Scythian horde
                    camped by Lake Maiotis
                where earth comes to an end

                        and, too, the flower of   600
                        Arabia: the wild

warriors who guard the steep
acropolis by Kaukasos,
a thunderhead bristling with spears.

The only other Titan I have seen
so trapped, so infinitely abused
was Atlas
god Atlas:
his awful strength
he mourns with his back.   610

The waves break
the surf moans,
the depths sound and sound,
the black
bottomless deep
hollows back,
and the pure springs of rivers and brooks
all for you

sorrow

PROMETHEUS   I say nothing, but don't think that means I'm   620
arrogant or stubborn.
I see myself abused, bullied, and . .
        Brooding
eats my heart away.
After all, who apportioned the privileges
        among these latter-day Gods?
            Who but I?
But I won't go into that,
you've heard it all before.
        Instead, hear   630
what wretched lives people used to lead,
how babyish they were—until
I gave them intelligence,
        I made them
masters of their own thought.

I tell this
        not against humankind, but only to show
how loving my gifts were . . .

Men and women looking
        saw nothing,   640
they listened
        and did not hear,
but like shapes in a dream dragging out their long lives
                bewildered
they made hodgepodge of everything, they knew nothing
                                        of making
            brick-knitted
        houses the sun warms,
nor how to work in wood.
They swarmed like bitty ants
        in dugouts   650
in sunless caves.
They hadn't any sure signs of winter, nor spring
                flowering,
nor late summer when the crops come in.
All their work was work without thought,
until I taught them to see
what had been hard to see:
                                where and when the stars
                                rise and set.

What's more, for them I invented   660
        NUMBER: wisdom
above all other.
                And the painstaking, putting together of
LETTERS: to be their memory
of everything, to be their Muses'
                mother, their
                        handmaid!
And I was the first to put brute beasts
under the yoke, fit them out
        with pack saddles, so they could take   670

the heaviest burdens off the backs of human beings.
Horses I broke and harnessed
    to the chariot shaft
so that they loved their reins, they showed off
the pride and wealth of their owners.
I, I alone invented
    the seawandering
        linen wingd
chariots for sailors.

All these devices, I invented for human beings.   680
Yet now in my own misery, I can't devise
    one single trick
to free myself from this agony.

CHORUS You've been tortured, humiliated, so that your mind
        wanders
driven to distraction.
Like a bad doctor fallen sick
    you grope, desperate
for what you can't find:
the drugs that will make you well.   690

PROMETHEUS But hear the rest, you'll be more amazed:
what arts, what
    resources I worked out!
And the greatest was this . . .
If someone fell sick
    there was nothing for it: nothing to eat, drink
nor rub into the skin.
Without drugs
people wasted away,
until I showed them how to mix   700
    soothing herbs
to ward off every sort of disease.

I marked out the many ways men might
    see into the future.

I was the first to realize what dreams are bound
to wake up: real.
And snatches of speech
         caught in passing, and chance meetings along the road,
these too have secret meanings.
I showed them this.   710
              And clearly analysed the flight
         of birds with crookt claws—
              what ones
                   bring luck, and which
              are sinister—
and the way each species lives,
what hates it has, what loves,
what others it settles with.
I looked into
         the silky entrails, I showed them   720
what color gall bladder meant the Gods were pleased,
and the liver's
         lovely marbled lobe.
And thigh bones wrapped in fat, and long backbones
         I burned,
I showed humans the pathway into an art
hard to figure.
I gave the fire
         eyes, so that its signs
              shone through   730
where before they were filmed over.

So much for these. As for the benefits to humankind
hid under the earth (the copper the iron
                        the silver the gold)
who but I could claim he discovered them?
No one, except a babbling idiot.

In a word: listen!
All human culture comes from Prometheus.

CHORUS Don't go out of your way to help humankind, yet
              neglect your own misery!   740

52

I'm hopeful, now, that once you're freed from these chains
you'll be powerful as Zeus.

PROMETHEUS Fate, that concludes everything, is not
                fated to make that happen—
not yet, not this way.
Ten thousand
                sorrows must wrench me. *That's* the way
                        I escape my chains.
Art is far feebler
than Necessity.   750

CHORUS But who swings the helm?
                                        who brings Necessity about?

PROMETHEUS The three bodies of Fate, and the unforgetting Furies.

CHORUS Is Zeus really less powerful than *these*?

PROMETHEUS Well . . . He can't escape His fate.

CHORUS But what *is* His fate, except to rule forever?

PROMETHEUS Don't be so insistent. You're not to learn that. Not yet.

CHORUS This secret must be awesome, you keep it so close . . .

PROMETHEUS Talk about something else!
It's not the time to speak out, not yet.   760
Whatever happens
the secret has to be kept,
            it's all I have
to escape this shame, this torture, these chains.

CHORUS (*dancing and singing an ode*)
                                May Zeus never turn
                                        His world
                                            wide
                                power against my mind

may I never
hesitate   770
to approach the Gods
with holy feasts
of blood drenched bulls
where Father Ocean, our father, streams and streams

may I never
say a sinful word

may this be ever
engraved in my mind
not melt
as words on wax   780

Nothing is sweeter
than life
lived
as long as this may be

always to hope
and feast, keep
the heart while it throbs
alive, lit up
with happiness
O but my blood runs cold, I'm cold, seeing you   790

raked over with
ten thousand tortures

you won't cower for Zeus,
you've a mind of your own
and you
honor humans

too much! Prometheus!

Tell us, what's the use of doing good
when there's no good in it
for you?   800

These things that live and die—
what help are they?
You must have seen
how blind and weak, like prisoners of a dream,
the human beings
are.
Can the plans of things that live and die
ever overstep
the orchestrated universe of Zeus?

This is what we've learned, Prometheus,   810
seeing your murderous
fate . . .

My heart flutters, I ache
to sing for you,
but not the song
I sang blessing your bridal bath and bed,
that bed you shared:
when
with gifts you courted Hesione
our dear sister,   820
persuading her, who gladly went home with you

(*Suddenly* io *bursts in: a beautiful young girl horned like a
heifer.*)

io (*chanting*)
Where is this?
Who lives here?
What is this
stormbeaten thing
yoked by rock?

Speak to me!
What did you do
to deserve this?
Where on earth   830
have I strayed to?

(*A sudden lowing shriek: it wells up through her, a voice
beyond her own, breaking out into wild unstructured
song.*)

again
it's the horsefly
it bites
my poor body!

No . . . it's the ghost of Argos
born out of earth
EARTH MAKE IT GO AWAY!
Herdsman I see
scaring me   840
with all his eyes!
He stalks by, the eyes give me
sly looks.
But he's dead! why can't the earth
hold him under?
From the dead dark he comes
to hound me
drive me
so that I starve
by the sands of the seashore   850

(*still singing, but in her own voice now, and less wildly*)

And always I hear the awful drone
the drowsy hum of reed-pipes bound in wax.
(*moaning, lowing*)   No
it's so far, where am I going?
Son of Kronos

you've yoked me to this misery,
what did I do wrong?
why this horsefly?
why this horror
driving a wretched thing out of her mind!   860

BURN ME WITH FIRE

BURY ME IN EARTH

LET ME BE SWALLOWED BY BEASTS OF THE SEA

I pray you, Master! I'm put through
my paces
enough now!
I don't know how
to get away from this misery.

Hear her now? Hear the girl
who's horned like a cow!   870

PROMETHEUS   (speaking quietly, as though to himself)
Of course I hear. It's the child of Inachos
driven by the horsefly.
Zeus was hot for her,
        Now she's hated by Hera
whose violence puts her through
these neverending paces.

    IO   (singing)
How do you know my father's name?
Who are you? Speak to the unhappy girl:
you, who
grieve as I do, how could you say   880
what my name is,
how could you know what winged disease from the Gods
stings me on? I'm near
eaten away!

57

(*bellows*)
              Tortured sick, hungry, I kicked up, came here

          STORMING STAMPEDED TERRORSTRUCK

          IT WAS HERA WHO BROKE ME

          HER SPITE BROKE MY SPIRIT

                    Who of all the unfortunate
                              suffers   890
                              as I do?
                    In plain words now
                    tell me: how much more must I endure?

                              Where's the cure? If you know
                              tell the wandering girl!

PROMETHEUS (*speaking*) All you want to know, I'll tell you,
              not weaving it into riddles
              but straight out: the right way
              to speak to a friend.
              You see the one who gave mankind   900
              fire:
                    Prometheus.

          10 (*speaking*) PROMETHEUS, patron of the whole human race!
                    Unhappy thing
              you suffer, what have you done?

PROMETHEUS A moment ago, I
                    . . . have ended the song of my suffering.

          10 Well, then, won't you grant me this other favor?

PROMETHEUS Name it. Ask me whatever you wish.

          10 Say who wedged you into this ravine.   910

PROMETHEUS   Zeus, with His will. Hephaistos, with his hands.

        IO   But the crimes you're paying for, what were they?

PROMETHEUS   No more! It's enough that I've told you this much.

        IO   Tell more! At what point
             does my wandering end, how long must I suffer?

PROMETHEUS   You're better off not knowing that.

        IO   What fate must I suffer? Don't hide it from me.

PROMETHEUS   It's not that I grudge you this gift.

        IO   Then why hold back? Why not tell it straight out?

PROMETHEUS   Not out of meanness.   920
                    It's just . . . I'm afraid
             I'll crush you with it.

        IO   Don't be kinder to me than I myself would like.

PROMETHEUS   All right, listen! If you insist, I have to give it to you . . .

    CHORUS   Wait, not yet!
             Let us
                 have our share of pleasure.
             Let's ask her
                 her disease,
             let's hear from her own lips   930
             what fate wastes her.
             After that, she can learn from you
             the ordeals to come.

PROMETHEUS   It's up to you, Io, to do them this favor,
             especially since they're your father's sisters.
             Then too it's worth troubling yourself

to weep over your fate . . . when there are others
who will weep with you.

10 I don't see how I can refuse you.
I'll tell you   940
all you want to know.
Although, even as I speak
    I'm ashamed, recalling
the storm the God let loose
       —my lovely body
          ruined—
and the One who drove it winging down
on me, wretched thing.

Always at night, haunting softspoken dreams
would wander into my bedroom   950
(where no man had ever entered)
whispering whispering
             "Happy, happy girl
you could marry the greatest One of all,
why wait so long
    untouched?
Desire's spear has made Zeus
burn for you. He wants to come
    together with you   960
making love.
Don't, dear child, turn skittish
    against the bed of Zeus. Go out
into the deep grasses of Lerna, where your father's
      cattle and sheep
         browse. Go,
so the eye of Zeus will no longer
be heavy-lidded with longing."

    Such dreams obsessed me
night after night. I was miserable.
Until, finally, I brought myself to tell my father   970
these dark-roaming dreams.

He sent many messengers off
                              to Delphi, and towards Dodona,
            to find out
      what he must do, what say
to please the Gods—
and they came back reporting
the shifty words of oracles,
            doubletalk
no one could make out.   980
At last, word came to father;
it was clear, and it was an order:
            "Drive her out of home and country,
            let her wander
                  untouchable, footloose
            to the far ends of the earth.
            If not, Zeus will fire His thunderbolt
                  down,
            your whole people
            will be exterminated."   990
Those were Apollo's oracular words.
Father gave in.
Against his own will
      as against mine
he drove, locked me out.
The bridle of Zeus
forced him to it.
            Suddenly
my body, my mind   1000
      warped,
my head
      horned—
            look at me!
Under the sharp bites of the horsefly
I kicked up, making
a mad dash for the sweet water
      at Kerchneia, and the spring
            called Lerna . . .
Suddenly Argos the earthborn herdsman

was following me: his rage the rage   1010
        of raw wine, staring with thick packt eyes
he crowded my every step.
            Until an unforeseen abrupt fate
cut him   from life!

Yet *still* the horsefly
goads me,
    the God's switch
lashes me land to land . . .

You've heard what was done.
Now tell me, if you can,   1020
the sorrows to come.
Don't for pity's sake
        try to warm me with lies.
To me, lies are the shamefullest disease.

CHORUS (*bursting into song*)

                    NO
                    NO
            make it go away!

(*individually*)

            I never dreamed I'd hear
            so horrible a story,

                such barbaric words   1030
            such pain,   such filth
        it's not to be seen, not endured!

                My heart's
                goaded stabbed
                iced

            It's FATE! your FATE!

                    Io
            I shudder at

62

PROMETHEUS Too soon you cry out! all brimming with fear!
            Wait: till you've heard what's to come.   1040

CHORUS   Go ahead, tell her. When you're sick it helps
            to know beforehand: what pain waits for you.

PROMETHEUS Your first appeal was not—for me—hard to grant.
            You wanted to hear this child
                recite with her own lips
            her own agony.
            Now hear the rest, what
                misery she's in for—
            this young girl, hated by Hera.

            You too, Io, daughter of Inachos,   1050
                take my words to heart.
            Then you will know
            at what point your journey ends.

            To begin: from here you must turn
            towards where the sun comes up.
            And walk on, across unplowed meadows,
                till you come to the roving Scythians
            who live in air, within reed huts
            on wagons with sturdy wheels.
            They're armed with long range bows   1060
            so don't get near them.
            Keep by the sea, let your feet
                trail through the surf
                    where the waves moan
            And so, pass through that country.

            To your left there'll be
            the Chalybes: those ones
                work iron.
            Watch out for them, they're savages,
            strangers can't approach.   1070

                              Next

you'll come to the Arrogangos, a river
that lives up to its name.
Don't cross though. It won't be crossed
      till you come to Kaukasos itself
            the highest of mountains: from whose very brow
the river in all its fury
gushes out.
Those peaks
      stand off among the stars, and those   1080
you must cross.

Head south then
till you find the man-hating
      army of Amazons.
One day they'll settle by the Thermodon, in Themiskyra,
where Salmydessos
      that haggard rockmouth of the sea, that
stepmother of ships, welcomes
sailors to death.
On your way, though, they'll help you   1090
and help you gladly:
                  you'll come to the Crimea,
            the isthmus
by the narrow gates of the lake.
But leave this behind: for with a strong heart
      you must cross that channel.
Channel of Maiotis now, but ever after
men and women will speak of your crossing:
they'll call it Bosporos,
      Place Where The Heifer Girl Crossed,   1100
in honor of you.

            But now you
have left Europe, you move on
            into Asia . . .

(*to the* CHORUS)
NOW do you see? This Dictator of the Gods

64

is violent in every way
    to everyone!
With this girl, this human,
    this God
wanted to make love.   1110
After *her*
        He drove this curse, this wandering.

Io, the suitor for your marriage
    has been a savage.
As for all you've just heard, believe me: it isn't even
the prelude to your song.

(io *cries out*)
        Howling and snorting again?
How will you take it, then, when you hear
the terrors to come?

CHORUS To come? You've more pain to tell of?   1120

PROMETHEUS A wintry sea of   sorrow.

IO Then what good's life? Why haven't I
thrown myself off this harsh rock,
smashed myself against the earth
    and so
        freed myself from *all* suffering!

Better to die once and for all
than drag out my days in misery.

PROMETHEUS   Then you'd be hard put
to bear this agony of mine.   1130
My fate is
    I cannot dic.
Death would be
freedom from sorrow, but now . . .

There's no end
  point to my misery, none
until Zeus falls from power.

10 Can Zeus ever, ever fall from power?

PROMETHEUS I suspect . . . you'd be glad to see that come about.

10 Of course I would, why not, isn't Zeus my oppressor? 1140

PROMETHEUS Then take it from me: these things are. They're so.

10 Who'll rob Him of His scepter, His power?

PROMETHEUS He'll do it Himself, through His own mindless schemes.

10 But how? Tell me, if there's no harm in telling.

PROMETHEUS He'll marry, and someday that marriage will trouble Him.

10 With a human being? a God? Tell me, if you may.

PROMETHEUS What difference does it make? Anyway, it's not to be told.

10 Who drives Him from His throne—His wife?

PROMETHEUS His wife. She'll bear a child greater than its Father.

10 And there's no way He can get around this? 1150

PROMETHEUS None . . . except, if I were freed from these chains.

10 But who's to free you against the will of Zeus?

PROMETHEUS As fate has it: one of your descendants.

10 What! You'll be freed from evils . . . by a child of mine?

PROMETHEUS Yes: the tenth, tenth then third, of the line following from
                                                            you.

IO You sound like an oracle: I can no longer follow you!

PROMETHEUS Don't, then, try to find out how far your sufferings go.

IO Please! Don't reach out a helping hand
            then take it back again!

PROMETHEUS I've two stories—I'll give you one of them.   1160

IO What are they? Tell me, let me choose between them.

PROMETHEUS Then choose. Shall I tell you in plain words
            what more you'll suffer, or who will set me free?

CHORUS Give her the benefit of one, please, and give
        us the other.
        You can't grudge us our fair share of the story.
        Tell Io
            how far she still has to go.
        Tell us
            who will set you free,   1170
        that's what we're dying to hear . . .

PROMETHEUS Since you're so anxious, I won't refuse to tell you
            all you want to know.
            First, Io, I'll tell you
                your wandering, whipt about like a top.
            Inscribe this in your mind's
            tablet, where memories are kept.

            Having crossed the stream between Europe and Asia
            —towards that dawnworld where the sun
                walks, flare-eyed—   1180
            you'll move on
                over swells of an unsurging sea.

These
    are dunes, it's desert!
You'll reach the Gorgonian flatlands, in Kisthene,
where the daughters of Phorkys live:
    three girlish hags
        shaped like swans.
Between the three, they've got
just one eye   1190
    and one tooth.
The sun doesn't ever
    beam on them,
nor will the night
        moon.
And their three sisters live nearby:
    repulsive with hair
not hair, they're wingd
        snake wool! it's

                    GORGONS!   1200
No human being will ever look on these and breathe
one breath more.

So much for the guardians of that land.

        Next comes
a horrible sight: Zeus's
    hunting pack, but sharp beakt, they don't bark
but lunge! They're GRIFFINS.
Avoid them, them and the one-eyed army
mounted on horseback, they're
    ARIMASPS   1210
by the River Wealth
rippling with gold . . .
    Stay away!

You'll come, then, to a land at the world's end
where tribes of black people live,
where the Fountains of the Sun
        gush

and the River Aithiops flows.
Follow that river's bank, till you come upon
sheer waterfall plunging   1220
            down from the Bybline Hills,
        hills bubbling
the sweet blessed waters of the Nile.
And he, that river, will lead you to
a three-cornered land:
            the Nile delta.
Io, here is your destiny.
Here, you with your sons
found your far off, long standing colony.

. . . If anything's obscure   1230
ask me again, and again
till it comes clear.
I've more spare time than I could wish for.

CHORUS   If you've left anything out, or if there's
                more to her disastrous wandering,
        why then tell her.
        Otherwise, grant what we asked.
        You remember what that was.

PROMETHEUS   She's heard the endpoint of her journey.
        She should know, too, that what she's heard   1240
                is true.
        I'll prove it.
        I'll tell her what agonies she went through
        to get this far.

(to IO)
. . . There's such a crowd of words
I'll skip most of them, and push through
to the endpoint of your wanderings.

After you had moved on
    to the Molossian meadows,

then to the sheer ridges   1250
      ranged around Dodona
(where Thesprotian Zeus
                is enthroned as oracle)
        you came upon
something incredible, wonderful: oak trees
        that spoke to you.
Without riddles, in luminous words
they saluted you:
(*his voice changing*)
                        You, who are to be the glorious
                                wife of Zeus   1260
Remember, Io? Doesn't this
nuzzle your memory . . .
        But then
the horsefly bit you,
        again
you bucked up, plunging along the coastal road
to the great Gulf of Rhea—
                        where suddenly
        you were stormed back in a blind rush.
Yet now and for all time, believe me,   1270
that inlet of the sea will be called
        Ionian,
all humankind will recall your passage there.

This then is proof: my mind sees
        more than may be seen.

(*to the* CHORUS)
Now—picking up the trail where I left off
        in my earlier story—I'll tell
you, and her as well,
what lies ahead.

Where Egypt ends, where silt   1280
        bars the mouth of the Nile
there's a city called Kanobos.

70

There I see
        Zeus . . .
He's bringing you back to your senses,
        stroking you
with a hand you no longer fear.
He merely
        touches you. Yet that's enough
to father your black child   1290
Epaphos (or Touchborn)
        who'll harvest
                as much of the land
as is watered by the broad flooding Nile.

The fifth generation following from him, a family of fifty
        girls will hurry against their will
back to Argos.
They want to escape
marrying their cousins.
But those men with their hearts worked up,   1300
        closing in on them
                as falcons on doves, will come hunting
a marriage that should not be pursued.
Yet the God will grudge them
the girls' bodies.
The Pelasgian earth
takes them in

when, daring
        during the nightwatch,
woman's war   1310
will make man a corpse.
She cuts
        his life out: tempers
her double-whetted blade, glowing red
in her lover's throat.
I wish my enemies could have
        such love made to them!
Yet one of the girls . . . *desire*

71

has her, spellbound.
He lies beside her, yet she cannot   1320
            kill.
In her, the murderous edge
goes blunt.
Her choice is
        she'd rather be called coward
than guilty of blood.
In Argos, your homeland,
that girl, your descendant,
will bear a line of kings.

That's another story, a long one, but I'll say this much: 1330
that from her seed
        a brave man will grow, a famous archer
who'll free me from these agonies.
This was prophesied by the Titan Themis, my mother
            born in archaic time.
She explained it to me.
It would take too long to say
how it will come about,
        and besides
it's of no use for you to know.   1340

10 (bellowing horribly: thrown back into the present, again
        becoming heifer, she breaks away chanting)
                    spasm! again
                    what manias
                    beat my brain
                    hot I'm hot
                    where's the fire?
                    here's horsefly
                    His Arrowhead
                    not fire forged
                    but sticks: heart
                    struck with fear   1350
                    kicks at my ribs
                    eye balls whirl

          spirally wheeld
          by madness, madness
          stormblasted I'm
          blown off course
          my tongue my tiller
          it's unhinged, flappy
          words words thrash
          dashed O at doom   1360
          mud churning up
          breaking in waves

                              (10 charges off)

CHORUS Wise, yes, that man was wise

     (*dancing and singing an ode*)
               who first weighed this in mind,
                    then shaped it
                      on his lips:
        "Marry your own kind, within your own class,
               there is no better way."
        As for people puffed up with money
            or the arrogance of birth,   1370
    no worker should want to marry the likes of those."

            Great Fates: never, never
                may you see
                 me coming
        to be the mistress in the bed of Zeus,
           nor would I be the bride
         of any God come out of heaven,
           I dread it: seeing Io's
    manshunning maidenhood driven wild by Hera.

     (*individually*)
                   For me,   1380
            when equals marry
             there's no terror.

What I'm afraid of is the Stronger Ones,
        what if their love
      should stare me down?
    There's no getting away.

    That would be a war that's not a war,
      where struggling more is more
            giving in.

    I don't know what would become of me,   1390
      I don't see how I could avoid
            Zeus's design.

PROMETHEUS As for Zeus, His heart's
        stubborn.
      But take my word for it, He'll be humbled yet.
      He's getting ready to marry
      ah, what a marriage . . . it will throw Him
          out of His throne and His tyranny,
      He'll end up nowhere.
              His father, Kronos, as he fell from his ancient throne   1400
          cursed Him.
      Zeus, then, will have consummated that curse.
      None of the Gods can show Him the way
          out of these troubles.
      Except me. I know these things
      and how they will happen.

      So. Let Him sit there, dreaming He's safe
          making sky high thunder, rattling
      a fistful of fire spurting rockets.
      Nothing will save Him from the sharp   1410
      plunge into shame,
              excruciating ruin.
      Even now, He Himself is working out the wrestler
      who'll take Him on.
      What an unbeatable
          wonder it is, this giant who'll discover

74

fire hotter than lightning, explosion
outroaring thunder!
As for Poseidon's three-pointed pitchfork
    that makes the sea heave and the earth quake,   1420
he'll knock it flying . . .
Stumbling up against this terror, Zeus will learn
what a difference there is: between
    being a power
and being a slave.

CHORUS   This curse on Zeus—it's only your own wishfulness!

PROMETHEUS   It *is* what I wish. But also, in fact, it's bound to happen.

CHORUS   You mean, we can expect someone to lord it over Zeus?

PROMETHEUS   Yes. And His neck will bend under worse pains than these.

CHORUS   Aren't you afraid, throwing such talk about?   1430

PROMETHEUS   Afraid? Why? I'm not fated to die.

CHORUS   He could make you suffer worse than this.

PROMETHEUS   So let Him! I know what to expect, I'm ready for it.

CHORUS   Those who are wise
                    bow down to the Inevitable.

PROMETHEUS   Honor! adore! go crawling before
whatever ruler rules
    today.
Me, I couldn't care less for your Zeus.
Let Him act willful, let Him lord it   1440
    this little while,
He won't lord it over the Gods for long.

                    (*out of the blue:* HERMES *appears*)
Look now, here's Zeus's errand boy,

special assistant to the new
   Dictator. No doubt
he's come to hand out some news.

HERMES You there!
    Yes,
you . . . are, I presume, the bitter, too bitter, intellectual
who committed crimes against the Gods,   1450
who gave their glory away
to things that live and die,
the one who stole
          our fire!

Well. The Father demands to know
   what's this marriage you're shouting about,
the one you infer
will depose Him.
A detailed explanation, please, and no doubletalk.
Don't make me come back a second time.   1460
In cases like this, as you're well aware, Zeus is not
inclined to go easy.

PROMETHEUS You've got an insolent
        pompous mouth,
you sound just like the Gods'
      puppet god.
You're all so young, newly in power, you dream
    you live in a tower
      too high up for sorrow.
Haven't I seen two tyrants   1470
thrown from that height?
And won't I witness the third, this latest
   God of the hour,
as He too falls?
It will be sudden, and most shameful.

Well? Do I seem afraid? Do I cringe
before the new Gods?
        Far from it. Not one bit.

Now scurry on back the way you came.
Whatever you ask, you'll get nothing out of me.   1480

HERMES Once before, by just such stubbornness as this
you came to moor yourself in these miseries.

PROMETHEUS Get this much straight: if I could trade
all my misery for your servility
I wouldn't.

HERMES Really. I suppose it's better to serve this rock
than be, say, Father Zeus's trusted
minister? His messenger god!

PROMETHEUS When you're insolent, that's the insult you're reduced to.

HERMES You seem to glory in your present situation.   1490

PROMETHEUS Glory in it? I wish my enemies such glory!
Including you.

HERMES Me? You blame me too for this disaster?

PROMETHEUS To put it simply: I hate all the Gods
who, when I helped them, wronged me.

HERMES You're insane, you're sick, and what you say is sick.

PROMETHEUS Agreed . . . if it's sick to hate one's enemies.

HERMES If you were doing well, you'd be insufferable.

PROMETHEUS (involuntarily, screaming his pain) AIE!

HERMES "Aie . . . ?" That's one word Zeus doesn't understand.   1500

PROMETHEUS (regaining composure)
Time, as it grows old, teaches all things.

HERMES   Really? But you still haven't learned to be sensible.

PROMETHEUS No, or I wouldn't be talking to a puppet.

HERMES   Then you won't, it seems, give the Father
            the information He demands.

PROMETHEUS Sure! Since I owe Him a great favor, on demand
            I'd be more than pleased to pay Him back . . .

HERMES   You're teasing me, treating me like a child!

PROMETHEUS But aren't you childish, I mean
                  sillier than any child, expecting me to tell you   1510
            anything?
            Zeus doesn't have one torture, not one ingenious device
            to pry this out of me—
            not till He eases
                  these shameful chains.
            Let Him rocket His lightning
                        the bolts trailing smoke!
            With white wings of snowflakes,
            with earth shattering
                  thunder,   1520
            let Him heave together everything there is
            in one confusion!
            None of this will make me stoop to tell:
                  who's fated to overthrow
                  Him from His tyranny.

HERMES   Think now: will any of this benefit your case?

PROMETHEUS I thought this out, and came to my conclusions, long ago.

HERMES   Come round, you fool! Consider what
            pain you're put through: come to your senses at last!

PROMETHEUS Why waste your breath? You might as well   1530
                  preach at the waves.

78

Don't think I'm so terrified by the will of Zeus
I'll turn womanish, turn
    my fluttering palms up, and beg the One I hate
to free me from these chains.
I'm a long ways from that.

HERMES All I say, apparently, I say for nothing.
I've begged you, and still
you haven't softened or mellowed:
but like a newly harnessed colt   1540
    you grind at the bit,
you buck, you fight the reins.
But really, this tactic you put such raving faith in
    is ineffectual.
When you're wrongheaded, it gets you less than nowhere
to be stubborn.

My words won't persuade you? Then think
what a storm, what a towering wave of ruin
    rushes down on you!
You can't escape it.   1550
First, the Father will flash
    lightning and thunder down, and pound
this jagged ravine into an avalanche
to bury your body in it.
Arms of stone will hug and hold you.
And so, you'll travel through the vast tracts
  of time. And at last
come back up into sunlight.
      Then
Zeus's feathered hound, the blood red golden EAGLE   1560
will tear your flesh
    into flapping rags.
It won't be invited, but it will come:
all day
    feasting, its beak
        stabbing your liver black.
Blood black.

79

At no point can you expect
an end to that anguish.
>   Until perhaps   1570
a God comes, willing to suffer
your pain for you,
willing to sink
>   down into lightless Hades and the dead dark
>   hollows of Tartaros.

Well, there you have it. Now make up your mind.
I haven't concocted a fiction, no bluff,
>   it's all too true.
Besides, Zeus cannot tell a lie,
He doesn't know how to.   1580
Whatever He says, it happens.
Now, Prometheus, give this careful consideration,
reflect on your situation.
Don't think it's better
to be stubborn, than to be sensible.

CHORUS   To us, it seems

Hermes has a point:
that you should give up your stubbornness, follow the trail
>   of good sound advice.   1590
Listen to him.
It's shameful for one so wise to be so wrong.

(music: from here on, all is chanted)

PROMETHEUS   Before he said one word
>   I knew what he would say!
>   Yet when an enemy's
>   hurt by an enemy

                                   why, there's no shame in that!

>   Let forkt lightning coil
>   down on my head

Let sky shudder thunder
with wind spasms   1600

Let hurricane shake
earth from its roots

Let waves surge and moan
as savages

            overwhelming the tracks
            high stars leave

Let Him hurl my body
utterly down

            the black pit
            of Tartaros, down   1610

            the stiff whirlpool
            Necessity . . .

Come what may: He won't
put *me* to death.

HERMES   These are the words, these are the dreams
of lunatics.
What part of this peculiar prayer
is *not* insane?

(*to the* CHORUS)   You, girls, who cry over his pains,
get out of here—   1620
before Zeus's lowing thunderclap
stuns you senseless.

CHORUS   Say something else, give us advice
we'll listen to!
We can't put up with this
aside, these words you've dragged up in passing.

How could you order me to be
a coward, how?
I'll suffer by his side
whatever comes, because I've learned to hate   1630

treachery: to me, the filthiest disease.

HERMES   Remember what I proclaim to you: when
doom hunts you down
don't blame your luck, don't say Zeus hurled you down
to unforeseen pain.

Not so. For you'll have brought this on yourselves.
There'll be no surprise
either, no tricks: for you'll be tangled up
within the boundless

net of disaster, and through your own madness.   1640

(HERMES *vanishes; the storm breaks out.*)

PROMETHEUS   No more words.
Now it's things.

Earth staggers to!
Rolling thunder
hollowing up
bangs at rock.
Lightning coils
gutter and flash!

Whirld winds suck   1650
up clouds of dust,
winds of the world
all dance around,
winds war winds!
Burning blue air
swirls up with
the heavy sea!

(*The* chorus *is gone*)

Out in the open
it's Zeus, it's Zeus
come down on me,
howling terror!   1660

MAJESTY OF MY MOTHER!
and of
SKY SKy Sky sky

wheeling your light
over us all,
watching all of
us, in common

see how I suffer,
how unjust this is

(*Blinding flash: blackout: howling darkness swallows rocks, all; until only the voice of* PROMETHEUS, *going back into the Greek it has come out of, rages still among the elements.*)

ESORAIS M' HOS EKDIKA PASKHO !   1670

NOTES TO THE TRANSLATON
APPENDIX
GLOSSARY

NOTES TO THE TRANSLATION

1-189 [The Prologue:] This falls into two movements. In the first, Prometheus is dragged in and chained, to the accompaniment of a dialogue between the coarse, sadistic Power and the pitying Hephaistos—both of them very clearly characterized by their language. Hephaistos leaves the scene after line 123, and Power does so after line 133, followed by the ever-silent policewoman, Violence. In the second movement (134-89) Prometheus, now entirely alone, speaks for the first time. For the unique metrical character of his speech, and its shifting attitudes to the future, see Introduction, page 13.

35-6 *the headlong . . . mother* In the Greek this is a single line, containing two massive compound adjectives; literally, "Of straightplanning Themis O steepthinking son!" An important contrast between the character of Themis (=Earth) and that of Prometheus is clearly implied by this, the first direct address to Prometheus in the play. How the contrast was worked out later in the trilogy we can no longer tell, but it is noteworthy that Earth appeared onstage in the play in which Prometheus was released, the *Unbound* (see fragment 3).

130 *The Gods called you "Resourceful"* There is a Greek word promḗtheia meaning "forethought," and the Greek noun-ending -eus often denotes an agent. To a Greek ear, therefore, the name "Prometheus" sounded like "fore-thinker" or "resourceful one." Here Power cruelly denies that even Prometheus' name has any meaning left in it.

173 *that perfume* The "odor of sanctity," an idea familiar enough to Christians, was also attributed by the pagans to supernatural beings. Compare, for example, Euripides' *Hippolytos*, line 1391.

176 *a mingling of the two* That is, something midway between god and man; to a Greek this will mean a demigod or hero.

87

190-283 [The entrance-song of the Chorus, and Prometheus' chanted responses.]
Just how the Chorus makes its entrance is an unsolved problem. The
ancient commentary discussed in the Introduction (p. 20) assumes
that the entire group is swung in on a crane, and remains aloft until
just before the appearance of Ocean (l. 431), when it descends and
disembarks. The wording of Aeschylus' text at line 192, literally
"with swift rivalries of wings," and lines 425-27, literally "leaving
my swift-rushing seat, and the bright sky, the holy path of birds"
presents further complications. Some modern commentators have
deduced from this that the Chorus was not merely swung in, but
swung in seated in a large winged chariot—or even in a flock of little
winged chariots, one to each girl, and hotly competing with each
other! We, however, prefer to suppose that the Chorus danced in on
foot in the usual way, with much use of mime, and that the "swift-
rushing seat" of line 425 is a metaphorical expression for their *imagined* station, hitherto, in the clear windy skies. Such a metaphor
would not be at all too violent for Aeschylus.

249-65 *My day will come . . . outrage* This is Prometheus' first allusion to the
Marriage-Secret (discussed in the Introduction, pp. 8-9), but it is as
yet expressed in very obscure language.

277-83 *He's savage . . . my friend again* Here only in the trilogy, so far as it has
survived, Prometheus foresees a total reconciliation between himself
and Zeus. See Introduction, pp. 15-17.

284-576 [The First Episode:] like the Prologue, this episode is in two movements.
In the first, Prometheus describes his part in the Titan War and its
aftermath, and stresses that he has given not only fire to mankind,
but also hope. In the second (ll. 431ff.), Ocean arrives and offers to
mediate with Zeus; but in vain.

431-576 [Ocean's intervention:] See Appendix, pp. 101-2, for the possibility that this
scene belongs to a sequence of element-scenes originally extending
through the trilogy; and Introduction pp. 20-21 for a discussion of the
manner in which Ocean's entry was staged. The tone in which this
scene should be acted has been a matter for much debate. On our
reading of it, the opening and close are almost comic. Ocean begins
with elaborate professions of friendship, and with much proverbial
wisdom, declaring that nothing will prevent him from going straight
to Zeus and arranging for Prometheus' release. He ends by departing

NOTES TO THE TRANSLATION

for his own home, on the not too convincing pretext that his monstrous steed is panting to return to the stable. His switch in attitude
seems to be brought about, above all, by Prometheus' terrifying
speech describing the physical power of Zeus, manifested in the
punishments of Atlas and Typhon. That speech is one of the most
majestic descriptive passages in all Aeschylus, and no doubt should
be delivered with an appropriate seriousness; during the rest of the
scene, however, we envisage Prometheus as impatient and slightly
sarcastic, Ocean as well-meaning but pompous and timid.

514 *Pity cut me . . .* For the following passage, see Glossary, ETNA and TYPHON.
Prometheus stresses the folly of Typhon in trying to oppose Zeus'
violence by yet more violence (notice the deliberate repetition in l.
519 and l. 526). *Knowledge* is the only possible weapon against the
physically omnipotent God, as the rest of this play will indicate.

577-619 [Choral Ode:] This simply constructed but powerful song moves from
the mourning for Prometheus of the Chorus itself, through the
lamentations of Asia and the tribes who dwell about the Kaukasos,
to . . . the howling of the water in the seas and rivers. Only one
stanza, lines 605-10 ("The only other Titan . . . with his back"),
interrupts its smooth progress, and that stanza is also the one passage of any length in the whole *Prometheus Bound* where the Greek
text given by the manuscripts is seriously corrupted. We have translated what we take to be the general drift of the partly unintelligible
Greek at this point: it is a lament for the sufferings of Atlas (cf. ll.
507-13) as he bears up against the weight of heaven. But this sudden
switch from Prometheus to Atlas as an object of sympathy violently
interrupts the sequence of thought. The problem has not yet been
solved to anyone's satisfaction, but in general there seem to be two
possible approaches to it: (1) the passage simply does not belong to
the original ode, but has been wrongly inserted in it; for example, a
quotation from some lost drama, written in the margin as a parallel,
was mistaken for part of the actual text by an early scribe. Or (2)
the corrupt Greek must be rather drastically emended. It is in fact
possible by such means to produce a text meaning "I have seen only
one other Titan so trapped in pain before now, . . . *and he too*
laments you," which would at least restore some coherence to the
thought.

595 *girls of Colchis* These are Amazons (see Glossary and also ll. 1083-89).

89

614 *the black bottomless deep hollows back*   Again, the Greek seems to have been corrupted here, but this time not so seriously. As given in the manuscripts, it reads "and the black abyss *of earth of Hades* hollows back." Following a hint by Wilamowitz, one of the greatest editors of Aeschylus, we have cut out the two expressions here italicized, assuming that both of them are separate (and unintelligent) attempts by early annotators to explain the word "abyss." In fact, the context suggests strongly that the "abyss" is that of the waters.

620-764 [The Second Episode:]   In two great speeches Prometheus describes how he brought the arts of civilization to mankind. The episode closes with a mysterious dialogue between him and the Chorus, in lines 739-64; see the note on those lines.

670 *pack saddles*   We have here followed the Dutch scholar Pauw, who emended the Greek word given in the manuscripts, *sōmasin* ("bodies"), to *sagmasin* ("pack saddles").

703-31 *I marked out . . . filmed over*   Prometheus here explains how he introduced the art of prophecy, enumerating many of its major ancient techniques: dream-interpretation; the interpretation of words overheard from passers-by; the interpretation of encounters in the street; augury, or the art of foretelling the future from the behavior of birds (711-18); extispicy, or prophecy through the examination of the entrails of sacrificial victims (719-23); and finally empyromancy, or the discovery of omens in the flames of the sacrificial fires, as certain parts of the sacrifice were burned. To a modern reader, the idea of prophecy as one of the civilized arts will seem strange, but two points are worth his consideration. First, the majority of ancient thinkers, lacking our data, supposed that the future of human affairs might be predicted by attention to the right phenomena, just as the future of the weather and of the starry sky could be (and still is) predicted. In that light, this discourse on prophecy makes good sense in the context. It is an important illustration of Prometheus' general theme, that he brought human beings from total inability to understand or control their environment, to full knowledge. Second, not all the techniques mentioned are obsolete even by modern scientific standards: Freud and others have taught us that at least the first two phenomena in Prometheus' list may actually provide some data for the understanding of a man's personality—and so of his destiny.

739-64 *Don't go out of your way . . . this torture, these chains* In this solemn
        passage Prometheus touches once more on the Marriage-Secret, and
        also approaches—as nearly as he ever does in the extant parts of the
        Prometheia—the question of who actually steers the destiny of the
        universe. Both topics are treated with a deliberate obscurity at this
        point. Later in the play, confronted with the appalling presence of
        Io, Prometheus will reveal far more of the Marriage-Secret. If the
        second question was ever answered in full, this must have occurred
        in some now lost passage of the trilogy, perhaps at its very end. Our
        only clues to Aeschylus' thinking, and uncertain ones at that, may
        be sought in the last play of the *Oresteia*, the *Eumenides*. In that
        play Zeus is faced by rivals in the government of the universe—
        again the Furies (and also their ancient sisters, the Fates). Only in
        the finale do the two parties reach an understanding, and so make
        possible a stable universe.

765-1392 [The Third Episode, and the Choral Odes on either side of it:] This
        long and crucial movement of the play, and its probable significance,
        are discussed in the Introduction, p. 10.

809 *orchestrated universe* The Greek word here, *harmonia*, is ambiguous—no
        doubt deliberately so—and we have tried to capture the ambiguity.
        Harmonia essentially means "a fitting-together," and would be ap-
        plicable to all sorts of processes, e.g., carpentry, government, and
        music. In its musical sense, which is common, it can mean "tuning,"
        "musical scale," or just "music."

813-21 In recalling the marriage of Prometheus with Hesione (also a daughter of
        Ocean), the Chorus introduces a major theme of this movement:
        sexual union. Here, however, the union is between equals, is brought
        about by *persuasion* (ll. 819-21), and is accompanied by the tradi-
        tional customs of an ancient Greek marriage—the bride-gifts, the
        ritual bathing and bedding, the hymenaeal song. In all this it con-
        trasts with the unions represented in the Io-scene and in the final
        choral ode.

896-1340 The spoken part of this episode is primarily concerned with the story of
        Io (see Glossary). This heroine, like Prometheus himself, seems to
        have preoccupied Aeschylus as she preoccupied no other Greek
        tragedian. In the *Suppliants* (between 466 and 459 B.C., perhaps
        463) she does not actually appear, but the Chorus of Daughters of

Danaos, who are her descendants, constantly appeals to her story. For them it is the supreme example of deliverance by Zeus at the end of long torments and wanderings. There is some reason to think that her story may have had the same significance in the context of the *Prometheia* as a whole; in the *Prometheus Bound*, of course, the main emphasis is laid on her sufferings at the hands of the Gods, but even here there is a prophecy of her final deliverance by an altered Zeus (see Introduction, pp. 15, 17).

The story is told almost, but not quite, in chronological order. Aeschylus begins at the beginning, with the tale of how Zeus fell in love with Io, and how she was metamorphosed into a heifer, narrated by Io herself (949-1018). Next Prometheus prophesies her wanderings from the place where he is bound to the border of Europe and Asia (1054-1104); and follows this by a prophecy of her journey through Asia and Africa until she reaches the Nile Delta (1178-1229). In his final great speech of this scene he looks out into the furthest future, from Io's healing at the Delta, through the return to Argos of her descendants, the daughters of Danaos, to his own release by her remote descendant, Herakles (1280-1333). But this culminating prophecy is prefaced (1248-73) by a brief account of her wanderings between Greece and the Kaukasos; thus the last gap in her story is filled in.

The geography of Io's wanderings, like the geography of the *Odyssey*, is baffling, once we pass beyond the area that was familiar to the Greeks and their navigators. Aeschylus seems not to have known, or—more likely—not to have cared particularly, just where lay the natural and supernatural terrors which Io was to pass through, before she reached peace in Egypt. What mattered to his poem were the terrors themselves which confronted the lonely girl at this troubled stage of the universe. All we can tell for certain is that Aeschylus has her wander in a clockwise direction from the peak in the Kaukasos, through part of what is now European Russia, into the far East and South, and finally up the Nile to one of its mouths at Kanobos (Canopus).

935 your *father's sisters*   Io's father is Inachos, a river-god of Argos. Rivers in general were thought of as sons of Ocean and Tethys (Hesiod, *Theogony* 337), and Aeschylus here implies the same parentage for Inachos (cf. the later mythographer Apollodorus, *Bibliotheca* 2.1.1, where it is explicitly stated). Thus Inachos is a full brother of the Daughters of Ocean and Tethys who form the Chorus.

985 *untouchable, footloose* The Greek adjective here used by the Oracle is *aphetos* (literally, "let-go"), which is a highly technical religious term, properly applied to animals consecrated to a God and allowed to, wander freely in his sacred precinct. Its relevance to Io is manifold. She is shortly to be turned into a quasi-animal, to be dedicated (in a sense) to Zeus, and to be sent roving across the world—His sacred precinct?

1072 *Arrogangos* The Greek name here is *Hybristes*, but no such river-name is found on any map, ancient or modern. There is a strong presumption that Aeschylus actually invented the name, just as he seems to have invented the Gorgonian Flatlands of Kisthene (1185), the River Wealth (1211), and the Bybline Hills (1221). If so, his intention here will have been to echo the names of actual rivers of the distant East (e.g., Araxes, Hydaspes), and at the same time to convey a terrible suggestion of violence—for *hybristes* is also a regular Greek word, meaning "violent," "insolent," or "lecherous." Our imaginary name tries to render these implications.

1085-6 *Thermodon . . . Salmydessos* For these place-names see the Glossary. As names, they are magnificently sonorous (one remembers similar geographical roll-calls, with similar effects, in Miltonic poetry), but the topography is disconcerting: Themiskyra is not close to the river Thermodon, and Salmydessos is on the opposite side of the Black Sea to either of them! Aeschylus, however, is thought to be indicating merely the general area in which, on his understanding, the Amazons would later settle. In Prometheus' present narrative they are located somewhere north of the Crimea.

1117-71 *Howling . . . dying to hear* Midway among the great solo speeches of the Io-scene stands this brisk dialogue between Prometheus, Io, and the Chorus. In it, for the first time in the play, Prometheus reveals two crucial prophecies in some detail, instead of alluding to them by vague and mysterious hints. Zeus, unless warned, will marry a woman whose child is fated to be greater than its father, and so will lose his throne; and Prometheus himself will be released by a descendant of Io's in the thirteenth generation. (As the Greek spectator probably knew, or guessed, that descendant would be Herakles himself. Herakles is never named in this play, even in the more specific prophecy at lines 1331-33. In the following play, however, the *Prometheus Unbound*, he appeared onstage, and fulfilled the prophecy.)

1182 *unsurging sea* The Greek text is very uncertain at this point. The manuscripts give various readings, none of them perfectly intelligible; we have here followed the suggestion of the French scholar Girard in reading *ponton peros' aphloisbon* at line 791 of the Greek. The resultant conception of the desert sands as a "surgeless sea" would be characteristic of Aeschylus, who loved such riddling expressions (there are examples in his descriptions of the Gorgons and Griffins, just below).

1239-1340 *She's heard . . . no use for you to know* In this, his last speech during the Io-scene, Prometheus' prophetic powers are shown at their most intense. His knowledge seems to crowd in on him (cf. l. 1245), and there is an immediacy and exactness of vision that is lacking elsewhere in his prophecies. The *truth* of this narrative of the far future is emphatically guaranteed in two ways. First, Prometheus employs a device which is also used by the prophetess Kassandra in Aeschylus' *Agamemnon* (ll. 1194-97), and is commonly employed by fortune-tellers to this day: to show his knowledge of the future, he recounts some events from his hearer's past (ll. 1248-73). Second, he refers to his wise mother Earth-Themis (1334-36) as his authority for the prophecy.

1295-1329 *The fifth generation . . . a line of kings* This story was treated, like that of Io herself (see note on 896-1340) in Aeschylus' *Suppliants*, and in the trilogy to which that play belonged; again—like so much in the Io-episode—it involves an attempt at love-making against the will of the beloved, a long journey in terror, and some kind of redemption at the end. It is further relevant to Io in that the girls concerned, her descendants, traveled back from the Nile Delta to her ancient home, Argos (thus completing a vast predestined cycle); and in that one of those girls was in turn the ancestress of the greatest of all heroes, Herakles.

Aeschylus here assumes a great deal of knowledge in his audience —knowledge which not every modern reader will share. In brief, the myth runs: the fifth generation of Io's descendants consisted of two brothers, Aigyptos and Danaos. The former begot fifty sons, the latter fifty daughters (usually known as the Danaids). The male cousins tried to marry the female cousins against their will, whereupon the girls, led by their father Danaos, escaped from Egypt to Argos. The males pursued them thither, and in the end a marriage was arranged between the fifty couples. On the wedding night, however, the indignant brides took revenge on their pursuers by stabbing them to death—all except one, Hypermnestra, who had come to love her partner Lynkeus. From this couple descended the royal line which culminated in Herakles.

1341-62 *spasm!* . . . *breaking in waves*   Io ends her scene as she began it: a maddened heifer, just—but only just—able to express her sensations in human language. Our translation attempts to bring out the great speed of this final chant, and the rapid succession of not quite coherent images. The imagery in lines 1358-62 is particularly uncertain; a literal prose translation of the Greek would run: "and muddied words thrash aimlessly against waves of grim doom."

1363-92 [The last Choral Ode:]   This short, low-keyed song, its detached deliberation contrasting with the violence of Io's chant just before, sums up the dominant themes of the entire Io-episode: equality and inequality in the union between the sexes, and the overwhelming terror of a God's love for an inferior. Both themes will recur in the scene that follows, but in a different context—Zeus' coming love for a woman whose name cannot yet be spoken (it is, in fact, Thetis), and the disastrous consequences.

1383-6 *what I'm afraid of . . . no getting away*   The Greek text is slightly corrupt, and several reconstructions in detail are possible. We believe, however, that there is little doubt about the general drift, as rendered here.

1393-1670 [The Exodos, or final scene:]   The last scene balances the Prologue in many ways. Both contrast with the central scenes of the play in the extraordinary rapidity and violence of their respective actions. In both, Prometheus is confronted by servants of Zeus, sent to execute the God's will. Both, in the Greek, show notable correspondences in phraseology and imagery. Yet all these parallels, in their various ways, only serve to accentuate the immense difference in the situation of the universe which has been brought about during the play. At the beginning, a lonely sinner was being chained in an apparently endless punishment, in the presence of the serene elements. At the end, a Titanic Prometheus confronts Zeus with the threat of dethronement, and all the universe is in turmoil.

1416-21 *this giant . . . knock it flying* This account of the unknown child who would be born if Zeus should marry Thetis is paralleled in Pindar's version of the legend (*Isthmian Odes*, VIII.34-5), where the child

"shall wield another weapon, stronger
than the lightning-bolt,
and than the unconquerable trident."

Yet at least one modern commentator (E. Beaujon, *Le Dieu des Suppliants* (Neuchâtel, 1960), p. 177) has had the fancy that the tremendous explosive force foreseen in Aeschylus' more vivid description is none other than the nuclear bomb . . . in which case the Child who will dethrone Zeus is, presumably, Man. This is a fancy only, but it seems worth a mention—there are, after all, uncanny insights elsewhere in the *Prometheus*.

1435 *the Inevitable* There is no precise English equivalent to the Greek word used here: *Adrasteia*, which is somewhere between the proper name of a rather impersonal goddess, and an abstract noun. We have chosen to render the latter facet of the word. The Goddess Adrasteia, who appears rarely in Greek literature, was identified with Nemesis, that divine power who remorselessly chastises human pride.

1443 *Look now* There is no clue, in the text or ancient commentary, to the manner of Hermes' entrance. J.S. suggests: *Feathery footsteps echoing as in a long corridor: Hermes appears.*

1470-1 *Haven't I seen . . . from that height?* Prometheus refers to the dethronements of Ouranos (Sky) and of Kronos.

1570-5 *Until perhaps/a God comes . . . Tartaros* Following hints in the Greek commentaries (see on fragments 1-3), we take this to be spoken in savage irony; Hermes implies "any God who tries to help you may expect the same punishment." Many modern commentators, however, see here an allusion to an obscure Greek myth, in which the Centaur Cheiron, in the agony of a mortal wound, offers to go down to Hades in Prometheus' place (Apollodorus, *The Library*, tr. J. G. Frazer (London and New York, 1921), vol. I, pp. 193 and 229-31, is the only ancient source). But this interpretation involves great difficulties, especially in the reconstruction of the *Prometheia* as a whole, and we prefer the simpler solution. There is a careful discussion of the Cheiron myth, and its problems, by D. S. Robertson,

"Prometheus and Chiron," in the *Journal of Hellenic Studies*, vol. LXXI (1951), pp. 150-55.

1640 **your own madness**   There is no indication in the text as to when Hermes exits, but this is the most likely point. J.S. suggests: *"Hermes takes off so rapidly he seems to vanish*

at once

utter disruption makes everything utterly clear, everyone knows who stands where."

1656 **the heavy sea**   Again, the text does not show when—or how—the Chorus exits. For the reason given in the Introduction, pp. 21-2, we have tentatively placed its disappearance here.

1670 *ESORAIS M' HOS EKDIKA PASKHO*   Literally, "you see me, how unjust things I suffer."

APPENDIX:
THE FRAGMENTARY
PROMETHEUS PLAYS

These "fragments" (the term as used here embraces any ancient evidence referring to the lost plays) have been preserved, practically, by blind chance. They are cited in the ancient sources for almost any odd purpose, *except* that of satisfying the literary critic's curiosity about the plot-mechanics or motivations of the lost plays. Galen, for instance, the great physician, has preserved fragment 8 of the *Unbound* merely as an illustration of an obsolete Greek word; and the geographer Strabo quotes fragments 5, 10, and 11 in connection with antiquarian and geographical problems of his own. Even so, the outlines of the *Prometheus Unbound*, at least, emerge with a fair certainty. The play began with the entrance of a Chorus of Titans, arriving to visit Prometheus, and chanting about the vast territories they had crossed to do so. (Already, then, it is to be inferred, the political atmosphere of the universe has lightened somewhat since the last play: Zeus must have relented from the dire punishment he imposed on the Titans in *Prometheus Bound*, ll. 326-29.) Prometheus, now restored to the light from his rock-prison, but suffering the torments of the eagle (all as Hermes had threatened, in *Prometheus Bound*, ll. 1551-67), gave the Chorus an account of his new sufferings. The long fragment 6, which describes these, may well be the most horrific passage in ancient drama; Prometheus seems very close to collapse. At an unknown interval after that, Herakles entered, and Prometheus delivered a speech, or series of speeches, in which he foretold Herakles' further wanderings. These would take him counterclockwise around half the world, first northwards through the freezing Russian winds, then westwards past the mouth of the Rhône, and finally (according to Strabo, in fragment 11) to the Garden of the Hesperides—which most ancient writers imagined as somewhere on, or near, the North African coast. This scene was thus a counterpart to the Io-scene in the *Prometheus Bound*, and completed a magnificent poetic survey of the entire world, as Aeschylus envisaged it. Herakles, like Io, will probably end his strenuous wanderings somewhere on the African continent. Either before or after this great prophecy (there is no evidence to indicate which), Herakles shot the eagle with his bow, and then, as fragment 14 shows, he released Prometheus, confirming the latter's prophecy to Io long ago. Yet fragment 14 also seems to show that the release was carried out before Prometheus and Zeus had been reconciled (compare, perhaps, *Prometheus Bound*, l. 1152, where Io is made to ask, "who's to free you *against the will of Zeus?*").

What happened next? The only remaining solid literary evidence is the brief fragment 15, which shows that mankind was at last reintroduced into the trilogy, as forever wearing the garland—a symbol of festivity—"as a recompense for [Prometheus'] chains." If this mysterious statement may be interpreted in the light of the two related (but not certainly Aeschylean) statements in "fragments" 16 and 17, we must conclude that Prometheus and Zeus eventually came to terms, but that Prometheus agreed to save Zeus's face by continuing to wear a chain of sorts—in the form of a garland! Recently some evidence of a quite different kind has been published, which seems to support this conclusion. It is an Apulian red-figure vase-painting, assigned to the third quarter of the fourth century B.C. (A. D. Trendall and T. B. L. Webster, *Illustrations of Greek Drama* [London, 1971], p. 61; here will be found a photograph, further references, and a discussion to which the present account is much indebted). At the upper center of the picture is Prometheus, a grandiose bearded figure, still fettered to his rocky chasm. At the left of him stands Herakles, with his club and bow: the Eagle is toppling, mortally wounded, into the lower register of the picture, which contains some female figures that seem to symbolize Hades. To the right of Prometheus stands a stately female figure, who might be Earth: and to the right again sits Apollo, the God to whom Herakles prays in fragment 13 of the *Unbound*. Most interesting of all, in view of our fragment 15, is the figure on the extreme left of the picture; here the goddess Athena sits quietly, as if waiting. She has her regular attributes of helmet, shield, and spear, but also holds up prominently, in her left hand, a very unusual attribute indeed: *it is a leafy garland*. There can be no reasonable doubt that this vase-painting bears some relation to the later scenes of the *Prometheus Unbound*. Unfortunately the ancient vase-painters very rarely reproduce a given scene from drama with literal precision, but tend to paint generalized views of the mythological situation concerned, often adding or substracting characters at will. The painting, therefore, cannot be taken as proving that all the figures shown were characters in Aeschylus' Prometheus Unbound. But at least it seems to confirm the indications of fragments 15, 16, and 17, that Prometheus was given a garland in exchange for his chains, and it may even add a highly significant detail—that none other than Athena, the favorite daughter of Zeus and the goddess of Athens, finally conferred this garland on Prometheus. Athena's specially close relationships both with Zeus and Athens, it will be noted, are celebrated in a great song of joy near the end of Aeschylus' Oresteia: Eumenides, ll. 916-1020 (above all in the stanza of ll. 996-1002).

At this point the evidence for the story told in the Prometheia finally gives out. It is useless to conjecture about the narrative of the final play, the Prometheus Pyrphoros; all that can be said with reasonable certainty is that its dramatic time was set later than the release of Prometheus (Pyrphoros, fragment 1). Yet there remains one further aspect of the trilogy to be considered, and that is the progress of the Elements through it. Prometheus' first utterance in the Prometheus Bound (134-39) is apparently a solemn appeal to the four elements—the deep bright sky (the Greek word is aithēr, often used for the element fire), the winds, the waters, and Earth. In the course of the action he is visited by the Daughters of Ocean, who form the Chorus, and even by Ocean himself (431-576); this first play is thus, in a sense, dominated by the watery element. Ocean's offer to intervene with Zeus, however, comes to nothing, for Prometheus' fearsome descriptions of the violence of Zeus eventually drive him and his monstrous steed back to the safety of home. The critics have never been able to make much sense of the Ocean episode in the context of the Prometheus Bound alone, and it is at least worth raising the question whether that episode may have been part of a chain of element-scenes, proceeding through the trilogy and only understandable in that greater context, if only we had it in its entirety. Certainly the final cry of Prometheus in the Prometheus Bound is an appeal to Earth and Sky alone—as if Ocean no longer counted? And in fact, one of the stage characters of the Prometheus Unbound was Earth herself (Unbound, fragment 3; compare, perhaps, the standing woman on the Apulian vase-painting mentioned above), while the Chorus consisted no longer of Ocean's Daughters but of Titans—who are the children of Earth and Sky (cf. the Bound, ll. 302-4). At this point, as so often in the exploration of the Prometheia, we are simply deserted by the concrete evidence. But the pattern established so far is striking enough; it suggests that there may have been a kind of elemental sub-plot to the trilogy, a ground-bass accompanying the melody of the Prometheus-Zeus story. One may speculate that the progression from Ocean in the first play through Earth in the second might imply the intervention of Sky (or aithēr, fire), in the final play. At least, that play's probable title, *Prometheus Pyrphoros* ("Prometheus Fire-Carrier"), contains that element in itself. But that is, admittedly, a speculation and no more.

We may now present our translations of the ancient evidence on which the above account is based. The fragment-numbers are our own, but for the convenience of any reader who may wish to refer to the original Greek and Latin texts we have added in square brackets the numbers which are used in the most recent edition of the fragmentary plays of Aeschylus: H. J. Mette, *Die Fragmente der Tragödien des Aischylos*, Berlin, 1959 (here abbreviated to "M"). Verbatim quotations from Aeschylus are translated in verse, and printed in italics.

"PROMETHEUS UNBOUND" FRAGMENTS

1-3: *General information about the play*
These three fragments are preserved in the Medicean manuscript of Aeschylus, in the Laurentian Library, Florence. It contains, besides the text of Aeschylus' seven surviving plays, a Greek commentary which was compiled in the classical period, evidently by somebody who was acquainted with much now-lost Greek literature—including the *Prometheus Unbound* and *Prometheus Pyrphoros*.

1. [M fr. 320] Medicean Commentary on *Prometheus Bound* (lines 743-45 of this translation). "That is: It is not yet my destiny to be released. For in the following play he is released, as Aeschylus indicates here."

2. [not in M] Medicean Commentary on *Prometheus Bound* line 759 ("Talk about something else"): "He reserves his words for the following play."

3. [M fr. 325] The dramatis personae of the *Prometheus Bound*, as given in the Medicean manuscript and several others, includes:

"EARTH;
HERAKLES."

Fragments 1 and 2 indicate that the *Unbound* immediately followed the extant play, and that in it Prometheus was released and probably mentioned the Marriage-Secret. Fragment 3 presents a strange problem. Neither Earth nor Herakles, of course, appears in the *Prometheus Bound*; but Herakles is known to have been introduced in the *Unbound* (see below, fragments 11, 12, and 14). It is therefore conjectured that Earth, also, appeared in the *Unbound*. Some early ancestor of our existing manuscripts may have contained both the *Bound* and the *Unbound* together, with a consolidated list of characters at the beginning; hence the accidental survival of these two names from the now lost play.

Fragments 4 through 7: the entry-chant of the Chorus of Titans, and Prometheus' speech to them

4. [M fr. 322] A Greek writer of the second century A.D., Arrian, writes in his *Navigation of the Black Sea* (ch. 19): "And yet Aeschylus in the *Prometheus Unbound* makes the River Phasis the borderline between Europe and Asia: in him the Titans say to Prometheus:

   > We come to see
   > these your sorrows, Prometheus,
   > and this agony of your chains . . .

   Then they tell how much country they have traversed:

   > . . . where the Phasis, the great
   > twofold boundary of Europe and Asia . . ."

   Here Arrian's quotation ends, but a little more information is given by the sixth-century A.D. historian Procopius, who mentions that Aeschylus placed this passage "right at the beginning of his tragedy" (*History of the Gothic Wars* 4.6.15).

5. [M fr. 323] The Greek geographer Strabo, who lived from about 64 B.C. to 21 A.D., says that the following passage occurred in the *Prometheus Unbound* (*Geography* 1.2.27):

   > "And the Red Sea's holy
   > flood with crimson bed,

and the Aithiopians' Lake
tendering food to all
—a coppery glitter
there, by Ocean's side—
where Sun, that sees all,
under the stroking of
the warm river revives
his tired horses, and
his own deathless body."

The quotation from Aeschylus in **5** is in the same meter (anapestic)
as that given in **4**, and it may reasonably be assumed to come from
the same entry-chant. The Titans, or some of them, will be describing how they have come from the uttermost south to visit the suffering Prometheus.

6. [M fr. 324] Cicero, the Roman statesman and philosophical
   writer (106-43 B.C.), quotes the following iambic verses as having been spoken by Aeschylus' Prometheus "when bound to the
   Kaukasos" (Tusculan Disputations 2.23-25, from a philosophical
   discussion on the endurance of pain). Cicero gives the lines in
   his own Latin verse-translation, but other examples of his translations suggest that he will have rendered the original Greek
   fairly faithfully.

"Titans
               blood brothers
                                  children of Sky
look at me! moored, chained
fast to the choppy rock—
     the way, towards nightfall, sailors in the howling narrows
        panickt
           secure their ship.
     In this way
Zeus, Son of Kronos, had me moored in iron.
Through Hephaistos' hands, His will became
        fact.
With cruel, painstaking craft, he slogged
   wedge   on   wedge
into me: splitting, sticking.
Thanks to that, I stand watch
mourning, at this castle of the Furies.

And always on the third day, for me, the light of day
is black,
when Zeus's horrible pet glides in at me—
                    the EAGLE
that digs in with crookt claws
gouging out
            her feast, until her crop's
bloated, rich with liver.
                    Then
screaming
            wheeling skyward . . . her tail feathers
drag through blood,
my blood.
And once again, my rag of a liver
                swells up like new, and again
the bloodthirsty banqueter comes back for more.
In this way
            I feast my prison warden:
who in turn, by deathless outrage,
tortures my live
            body—
look! Zeus's chains
clench me, I can't
            protect my chest from that
filthy thing.
Only, myself
            gutted, take what
agony comes, grope for an end to pain
and burn, like sex, for death.

But by the will of Zeus
I'm exiled far away from death.
Century has swarmed on shuddering
                    century
around this old anguish, this
wedge through my body

whose drops of blood
            melted in the flaming sun
over Kaukasos, rain
endlessly on rock."

Fragment 6, though its position in the play is not stated by Cicero, may well come from Prometheus' answer to the entry-chant of the Titans.

7. [M fr. 336a] Plutarch, the Greek essayist and biographer (*fl.* ca. 100 A.D.), discussing mankind's dominance over the other animals in his essay *On Fortune*, writes: "According to Aeschylus, Prometheus—that is, Reason—is responsible, for he

> gave horse and donkey and the breed of bulls
> to be as slaves to us and bear our burdens."

Fragment 7, to judge by its strong resemblance to lines 668-75 of the *Bound*, may also have belonged to a speech made by Prometheus to the Titan-Chorus further describing his benefits to man. This, however, is not certain, since Plutarch does not expressly attribute his quotation to the *Unbound*.

Fragments 8 *through* 12: *Prometheus foretells the wanderings of Herakles in the north and west*

8. [M fr. 327] Galen, the famous Greek physician who lived from ca. 129 to 199 A.D., writes in his *Commentary on Hippocrates' Epidemics*, 6.1.29, that he found the following iambic lines in Aeschylus' *Prometheus Bound* (sic: this is either a slip for "Unbound," or Galen is using "Prometheus Bound" as a generic title for the whole trilogy):

> Follow straight along this pathway.
> You'll come, first, to the high winds
>   of Boreas.
> Take care:
>   for fear
> the hurricane with its wintry blasts
> will howl down
> whirling you into the sky."

9. [M fr. 329] Stephanos of Byzantium, a Greek geographical writer who is thought to have lived in the fifth century A.D., quotes the following iambic lines on the Scythian tribe *Gabioi*, from "Aeschylus in the *Prometheus Unbound*":

> "You'll arrive, then, at a just
> community, more just than any other

and friendlier.
>> These are the Gabioi.
> Here, no plow, nor any hoe
>> hacks at the land
> but the plains plant themselves,
> the harvest is endless."

10. [M fr. 328] Strabo (on whom see fragment 5) writes as follows in his Geography 7.3.7.: "Aeschylus concurs with Homer [Iliad 13.4-6] in saying about the Scythians,

> But Scythians, well-governed,
>> who feast
> on maresmilk cheese . . ."

11. [M fr. 326a] Strabo (on whom see fragment 5) discusses in the fourth book of his Geography the scientific problem presented by a pebble-strewn plain which lies in southern France between the Rhône estuary and Marseilles. He mentions (4.1.7) a mythical explanation of the phenomenon in the following words. "In (Aeschylus) Prometheus, advising Herakles about that journey of his from the Kaukasos to the Hesperides, says:

>> You'll come upon
> the Ligyes, a horde
> that doesn't know what fear is.
> Fierce a fighter as you are, you won't fault
>> their fighting.
> As fate has it: you'll run out of weapons,
> you can't grab even
>> one stone off the ground
> because the plain is soft, it's
> dust.
>> But Zeus will see you
>>> bewildered there
> and pity you, and cast a stormcloud
>> to shadow the earth
> in a flurry of rounded rocks.
> You'll heave them, and with ease
> batter the Ligyan horde back."

12. [M fr. 326c] Hyginus was a Latin mythological writer who drew heavily on Greek sources, especially tragedy; his date is uncertain, but he may well have lived in the second century A.D. In his *Astronomy in the Poets*, 2.6, he discusses the myth underlying the constellation called *Engonasin* (*Hercules* in modern star-maps), in the following words:

"But Aeschylus in the play entitled *Prometheus Unbound* says that Herakles is not fighting with the Dragon, but with the Ligyes. His story is that at the time when Herakles led away Geryon's cattle he journeyed through the Ligyan territory. In trying to remove the cattle from him they came to blows, and he pierced a number of them with his arrows. But then his missiles gave out, and after receiving many wounds he sank to his knees, overpowered by the barbarian numbers and by the failure of his ammunition. Zeus, however, took pity on his son, and caused a great quantity of rocks to appear around him. With these Herakles defended himself and routed the enemy. Hence Zeus set the likeness of him, fighting, among the stars."

Fragments 11 and 12 clearly refer to the same passage of Aeschylus, and fragment 12 proves that that passage occurred in the *Unbound*. It is extremely likely that 8 and 9 also belong to Prometheus' prophecies of Herakles' wanderings. Fragment 10 is attributed only conjecturally, on the ground that it, too, refers to the great Russian land mass and its inhabitants.

Fragments 13 and 14: Herakles rescues Prometheus

13. [M fr. 332] Plutarch (on whom see fragment 7) discusses in his dialogue *Amatorius*, 757E, how various Gods are invoked for various purposes. In the course of the discussion he remarks: "But Herakles invokes a different god when he is going to raise his bow against the bird, as Aeschylus says—

    Let Hunter-Apollo level straight this shaft!"

14. The same Plutarch begins his *Life of Pompey the Great* by commenting on the contrast between Pompey's popularity and the extraordinary hatred felt for his father, Pompeius Strabo. The opening words of the *Life* run: "From the first the Roman people seems to have felt towards Pompey as Prometheus in Aeschylus feels towards Herakles when, after being rescued by him, he says—

    This dearest child of
    the Father I hate!"

Although Plutarch does not name the play from which he is quoting in fragment **13**, the only known mythological situation which the quotation would fit, among the lost works of Aeschylus, is the shooting of the eagle in the *Unbound*. The Apulian vase discussed above (pp. 100-101) perhaps lends further support to the attribution. Fragment **14** must certainly refer to the *Unbound*; its implication that Prometheus continued to hate Zeus even after the rescue is noteworthy.

Fragments 15 through 17: the Garland of Prometheus

15. [M fr. 334] Athenaeus, an enormously learned Graeco-Egyptian scholar, compiled his *Deipnosophistae* in about 200 A.D. In Book 15, p. 674 D of that work, during a discussion of the custom of wearing garlands, he writes: "Aeschylus in the *Prometheus Unbound* expressly says that it is in honor of Prometheus that we put the garland about our heads, as a recompense for his chains."

16. [also M fr. 334] Another passage from the same discussion by Athenaeus (Book 15, p. 672 F); here he is quoting a story from an earlier historian, Menodotos, concerning a strange penalty laid upon some ancient inhabitants of the isle of Samos: "Apollo through his oracle told them to pay that penalty which in times gone by Zeus laid upon Prometheus for his theft of fire. For after Zeus released him from those most cruel chains, Prometheus consented to pay a voluntary but painless requital; and this is what the Leader of the Gods ordained that he should have. Whence it was that the garland was revealed to Prometheus, and not long afterwards it was inherited by mankind also, whom he had benefited by the gift of fire."

17. [not in M] Hyginus (on whom see fragment **12**), *Astronomy in the Poets* 2.15, writes as follows: "Several people have said that he (Prometheus) wore a garland in order that he could say that he had been the victor, since he had sinned without being punished for it; and for that reason mankind began the custom of wearing garlands in moments of their greatest joy, and in victories."

Fragment **15** alone attributes the story of the garland expressly to Aeschylus. We have tentatively included **16** and **17** because they seem to throw a little further light on the brief statement given in **15**, and because it is possible that the solution which they indicate could have originated, in outline, with Aeschylus. The vase-painting discussed above, pages 100-101, also suggests that a garland was somehow associated with Prometheus' release in the *Unbound*.

THE FRAGMENTS OF THE "PROMETHEUS PYRPHOROS" ("FIRE-CARRIER")

1. [M fr. 341] The Medicean Commentary (for which see the note on fragments 1-3 of the *Unbound*) has the following note on *Prometheus Bound* line 144 ("ten thousand years"): ⟨That is,⟩ many years; for in the *Pyrphoros* (Aeschylus) says that (Prometheus) has been bound for thrice ten thousand years."

2. [M fr. 351] Aulus Gellius, a Roman literary scholar of the second century A.D., quotes the following line from "Aeschylus in the *Prometheus Pyrphoros*" in his *Noctes Atticae*, 13.19.4:
   "Quiet, where need is; and talking to the point."

3. [M fr. 340] In the Medicean manuscript of Aeschylus (for which see the note on fragments 1-3 of the *Unbound*), and two other manuscripts, there is included an extensive catalogue of the plays of Aeschylus, which must go back to classical times. Among the titles there given occurs:

   "PROMETHEUS PYRPHOROS."

Those three fragments are the only classical evidence we now have about the *Pyrphoros*. Fragment 1 seems to show that the action took place later than that of the *Bound*; 3 simply confirms that the play was once in existence; 2 (as a devoted student of Aeschylus, George Thomson, once remarked) offers excellent advice to would-be reconstructors of its plot.

GLOSSARY

of names that occur in the Prometheus Bound and in the Fragments

Note: in the Prometheus plays, Aeschylus shows a strong tendency to free invention with regard to mythological data and to geographical names. In compiling this glossary, we have therefore relied primarily on the information given in Aeschylus' own text. Where that has failed, we have had recourse primarily to Hesiod (whose works Aeschylus knew) and to Herodotus (who wrote not very long after Aeschylus' death) in order to fill in the mythological and geographical details respectively. In such cases, of course, one cannot always guarantee that the resulting picture was the picture envisaged by Aeschylus, but it is the best that can be given in the circumstances.

AITHIOPIANS, a generic Greek name for the peoples who inhabited the unknown southern parts of the earth. Aeschylus seems to have thought that they extended even as far as India (*Suppliants*, 284-86).

AITHIOPS, a river, imagined by Aeschylus to be in the furthest South.

AMAZONS, a tribe of female warriors, who occur in Greek poetry from Homer's *Iliad* onwards. Herodotos (*Histories* IV.110-17) still takes them for a historical people, and places their descendants east of the Sea of Azov. They were renowned for their fierce use of the axe and the bow, and for their contempt of males, with whom they would associate only for child-bearing purposes.

APOLLO, an Olympian God, son of Zeus and Leto. In the *Prometheus* he is mentioned only in his capacity as the oracular God of the shrine at Delphi.

ARGOS (1), a miraculous being, covered with eyes all over his body, but otherwise of human shape. In the *Prometheus* Aeschylus calls him a child of Earth. Argos was ordered by Hera to guard Io after the latter had been turned into a heifer, but was soon after slain by Hermes.

(2), an ancient city in the northeast Peloponnese, and the home of Io.

ARABIA, usually thought of by the Greeks as lying in the area now called Saudi Arabia. Aeschylus, however, in the text we have, appears to place some Arabians in the neighborhood of the Kaukasos as well.

ARIMASPS, a fabulous race of one-eyed men, placed by Aeschylus somewhere in the far East. Herodotos reports a story (which he himself refuses to believe) that the Arimasps' occupation consisted in stealing gold from its monstrous guardians, the Griffins (q.v.): Book III, ch. 116, and Book IV, ch. 13.

ARROGANGOS River: our punning translation of Aeschylus' fictitious river-name, HYBRISTES. See note on line 1072.

ATLAS, a brother of Prometheus. In Hesiod (Theogony 517-19, 745-46), Atlas is punished by being made to bear the sky on his shoulders, somewhere in the far West. In the Prometheus his punishment is not clearly explained, but it seems to consist of propping up a presumably unstable pillar which separates the earth from the sky.

BOREAS, God of the North Wind.

BYBLINE HILLS, a fabled range in the far South, first heard of in Aeschylus, and perhaps invented by him on the basis of the word byblos (= the Egyptian papyrus). Here he locates the springs of the Nile.

CHALYBES, a tribe somewhere in the East, to whom the Greeks attributed the first working of iron. Some historical reality no doubt underlies the vague legends; Xenophon, in his great march through Asia Minor, actually fought with a tribe of this name. But the Greek poets generally are uncertain about the whereabouts of the Chalybes. In Aeschylus' account they seem to dwell somewhere north of the place where Prometheus is bound.

CILICIA, a territory on the southeast coast of Asia Minor, where the monster Typhon (q.v.) dwelled.

COLCHIS, a city at the eastern end of the Black Sea.

CRIMEA (Greek Isthmos Kimmerikos, whence the modern name is derived).

DELPHI, a town in central Greece, famous for its sanctuary and oracle of Apollo.

DŌDŌNA, an ancient sanctuary of Zeus, in the far north-west of Greece. The shrine lay in a valley of the Molossian hills, east of the region named Thesprotia, and was famous above all for its oracles, supposedly delivered by speaking oak-trees.

EARTH (Greek Gaia or Gē), wife of Sky; the couple, according to Hesiod, were the first divine pair to rule the Universe. In the *Prometheus Bound*, Earth is represented as the mother of Prometheus, and is also identified with the goddess Themis ("Right").

EPAPHOS, son of Io, miraculously conceived by the touch of Zeus in the Nile Delta. He became ruler of Egypt, and ancestor of a line of kings. (Many Greek writers identified him with the Egyptian bull-god Apis, but this identification is not mentioned in the *Prometheus*.)

ETNA (Greek Aitna), the volcanic mountain in northeast Sicily; its spectacular eruption in (probably) 479/8 B.C. is alluded to both in the *Prometheus* and in Pindar's First Pythian Ode. Both poets imagine that Typhon (q.v.) is buried below the mountain, and responsible for its fires.

FATES (Greek Moirai), the three goddesses who are in charge of destiny. In Hesiod they are the daughters of Night, and their names are Klōthō, Lachesis, and Atropos.

FURIES (Greek Erinyes), a group of ancient goddesses of indeterminate number, who in most Greek writers are primarily concerned with the punishment of blood-guilt and the enforcement of oaths. Both in the *Prometheus* and in the *Eumenides* (where the Chorus consists of Furies), Aeschylus attributes to them great influence in the affairs of the universe.

GABIOI, a Scythian tribe, already renowned for their justice in Homer (*Iliad* 13.6, where they are called Abioi).

GORGONIAN FLATLANDS, a geographical name apparently coined by Aeschylus from the name "Gorgons" (q.v.). He places them in the far East.

GORGONS, three monstrous snake-haired sisters, the most famous of whom is Medusa. Aeschylus places their home in the far East. He does not give their parents' names, but according to Hesiod these were Phorkys (q.v.) and Kētō.

GRIFFINS "are beasts which are like lions, but have the wings and beak of an eagle" (Pausanias, *Description of Greece* I.24.6). Herodotos has heard legends that these monsters dwell in the far North or Northeast, guarding great quantities of gold, which the Arimasps (q.v.) are forever trying to steal from them (Herodotos III.116, IV. 13). Aeschylus seems to place them in the far East or South.

HADES, a God, brother of Zeus and ruler of the world of the dead below the earth. In English usage—which we have followed— the name is often used to mean that world itself.

HEPHAISTOS, an Olympian God, borne by Hera without intercourse with Zeus. He is always represented as lame, but he is the great craftsman of the Gods, famed above all for his metal-work.

HERA, daughter of Kronos and Rhea, wife of Zeus, and queen of the Olympian Gods.

HERAKLES, son of Zeus and Alkmēnē, through whom he was descended, in the thirteenth generation, from Io. He was the greatest of all Greek heroes; among his many labors was the freeing of Prometheus.

HERMES, an Olympian God, son of Zeus and Maia. The chief among his many functions is that of Herald to the Gods.

HĒSIONĒ, a daughter of Ocean, and wife of Prometheus.

HESPERIDES: these nymphs (their name means "girls of the West," or "girls of the Evening") kept eternal watch over a garden in which grew golden apples. Hesiod places them in the far West, in the neighborhood of Atlas.

INACHOS, son of Ocean, and father of Io; he gave his name to the River Inachos, near Argos (2).

IO, daughter of Inachos. Her story, as envisaged by Aeschylus, is given in full in the *Prometheus* and (with some differences in detail and emphasis) in the *Suppliants*. In brief: Zeus fell in love with her; she was turned into a heifer, and Hera set the many-eyed Argos (1) to watch over her; Argos was slain by Hermes; whereupon Hera sent the horsefly to torment Io, and drive her over the earth. In the course of her wanderings she came to Prometheus, who, in the play of that title, prophesies her future fate.

IONIAN SEA: this name is usually given to the stretch of sea between the west coast of Greece, the "foot" of the Italian peninsula, and Sicily; but some Greek writers, including (apparently) Aeschylus, extend it to the entire Adriatic.

KANŌBOS, better known as Canōpus, a city on the Egyptian coast some fifteen miles east of what was later Alexandria.

KAUKASOS, the mountain range east of the Black Sea, which was the scene of Prometheus' punishment. Greek writers, even long after Aeschylus, believed this range to be of vast extent: Strabo, the great geographer who wrote in the early first century A.D., criticizes some of them for believing that it reached "from the mountains overlooking Colchis and the Black Sea to the mountains of India, and the eastern ocean that borders on them" (Strabo XI. 507). Aeschylus seems to imagine Prometheus as being chained on one of the lower peaks of the range, some distance from the great peak which he calls "Kaukasos itself," and which Io must cross in her later wanderings.

KERCHNEIA, a small town some fifteen miles southwest of Argos (2), and in its territory; here was a spring of fresh water.

KISTHĒNĒ, a far Eastern place-name, first found in Aeschylus and perhaps invented by him.

KRONOS, youngest son of Earth and Sky, husband of Rhea, and king of the Titans. He has been conquered by Zeus, dethroned, and imprisoned in Tartaros.

LERNA, a coastal region of the territory of Argos (2), famed for its spring-water.

LIGYES, better known by their Roman name of "Ligurians," a people who inhabited the territory which is now the southeast corner of France and the northwest corner of Italy.

MAIOTIS, Lake, the inlet of the Black Sea east of the Crimea; now the Sea of Azov.

MOLOSSIAN (Meadows), see Dodona.

OCEAN (Greek Okeanos), son of Earth and Sky according to Hesiod (Aeschylus does not name his parents); husband of Tethys, and father of the girls who compose the Chorus in the Prometheus (see next entry). He is both a God of the Titan-generation, and a river—the greatest of all rivers, encircling the world.

OCEAN, DAUGHTERS OF: in Hesiod, Ocean marries Tethys and begets many water-nymphs; after naming a large number of them, the poet adds, "but there are many others, also; for there are three thousand slender-ankled daughters of Ocean, scattered far, taking care everywhere alike of the land and the depths of water, children glorious among goddesses." Of some of these, the Chorus of the *Prometheus* is composed.

PELASGIA, an ancient name for Greece, and especially for the region around Argos (2), derived from the name of a legendary ruler, Pelasgos.

PHASIS, a river running into the eastern end of the Black Sea, by Colchis.

PHORKYS, DAUGHTERS OF, three monstrous and aged sisters, who possessed only one eye and one tooth between them—which they used by turns. They are better known as the "Graiai." According to Hesiod their mother was Kētō, so that they were full sisters of the Gorgons (q.v.).

POSEIDON, an Olympian God, son of Kronos and Rhea. To the classical Greeks he was not only God of the sea and its storms, but also God of earthquakes; in both capacities his weapon is the three-pronged fork, the trident.

PROMETHEUS, in Aeschylus' play, is the son of Earth-Themis (q.v.); his father is not named; his wife is Hesione, one of the daughters of Ocean.

RHEA, wife of Kronos (q.v.). The *Gulf of Rhea* is Aeschylus' name for the upper Adriatic.

SALMYDESSOS, a city on the southwest coast of the Black Sea, about sixty miles west of the Bosporus.

SCYTHIA, a vast tract of country, its outer limits undefined, but roughly co-extensive with European Russia. An elaborate account of the land and its many tribes (generically called the Scythians), as the fifth-century Greeks knew them, is given in Herodotos' *Histories* IV. 1-82.

SKY (Greek Ouranos), consort of Earth, and also (according to Hesiod) her parthenogenetic son. The two together were the first divine sovereigns of the universe.

TARTAROS, the lowest and darkest depth in the universe, below Hades itself. Here Zeus imprisoned the defeated Titans and Kronos,

hurling them (according to Hesiod) "as far below the earth
as sky is above earth—*that* is the distance from earth to the
dark mists of Tartaros."

TĒTHYS, wife of Ocean (q.v.).

THEMIS, whose name means "Right," is identified with Earth (q.v.)
in the *Prometheus Bound*. Elsewhere in Greek literature—
even in Aeschylus' *Eumenides*—she is an independent Goddess, a daughter of Earth and Sky, and thus a sister of Kronos.

THEMISKYRA, a town on the south coast of the Black Sea.

THERMŌDŌN, a river running into the Black Sea on its southern coast.

THESPRŌTIA, see Dodona.

TITANS, the name for the race of ancient deities who were born of
Sky, and rebelled against him under the leadership of their
youngest brother, Kronos. They in turn were deprived of
their power by the following generation, the Olympian Gods,
led by Zeus.

TYPHON (or Typhoeus), according to Hesiod, was the youngest child
of Earth, begotten on her by Tartaros. A monstrous being, he
rose up against Zeus after the latter's defeat of the Titans,
and was destroyed by the thunderbolts in a fearful battle
(*Theogony* 820-80). Aeschylus follows this account in the
main, but adds that Typhon's body was buried under Mount
Etna.

WEALTH (Greek Ploutōn), a river in the far East, apparently invented by Aeschylus.

ZEUS, ruler of the Olympian Gods, youngest son of Kronos and
Rhea, husband of Hera. At the dramatic date of the *Prometheus Bound*, Zeus has only recently defeated the older divine
generation of Titans, and established his new régime.